THE ART OF THE POLITICAL DEAL

*How Congress Beat the Odds
and Broke Through Gridlock*

JILL LAWRENCE

FOREWORD BY NORMAN ORNSTEIN

Most of the material in this book was first published by the Brookings Institution in an online series called "Profiles in Negotiation." Brookings and Elaine C. Kamarck, senior fellow in the Governance Studies Program at Brookings and founding director of its Center for Effective Public Management, played a central role in the creation of this work. Some material was also published previously by *Politico Magazine*.

ISBN: 9781520480169

Cover photo: The U.S. Capitol at sunrise, kropic1/Shutterstock.com

PRAISE FOR *THE ART OF THE POLITICAL DEAL*

"This is legislative sausage-making that you do, in fact, want to see. Jill Lawrence provides a fascinating behind-the-scenes look at how the hard work of legislating, compromise and consensus-building actually unfolds on Capitol Hill—and demonstrates that the process can, and sometimes does, produce results."

—Former Senator Olympia Snowe, Republican of Maine, a senior fellow at the Bipartisan Policy Center and co-chair of its Commission on Political Reform

"This book could not be more timely. Into our hyper-polarized political scene comes Jill Lawrence, showing with real cases how negotiation can actually get things done even in the context of two parties who are more at odds than at any time in the last 100 years. These cases are not only insightful about the dynamics of negotiation in Congress, they are also beautifully readable—actual page-turners. Highly recommended."

—Jane Mansbridge, Adams Professor of Political Leadership and Democratic Values at Harvard's Kennedy School of Government and co-editor of *Political Negotiation: A Handbook*

"Are you looking for a ray of hope at a time of gloom and doom about poisonous partisanship? If so, you need to read Jill Lawrence's The Art of the Political Deal. *When the big players want to work across the aisle to get something done in the national interest, they still can. Lawrence gives us concrete examples from the recent past in a well written, enlightening narrative."*

—Larry Sabato, director of the University of Virginia Center for Politics and author of *The Kennedy Half-Century: The Presidency, Assassination, and Lasting Legacy of John F. Kennedy*

"The Art of the Political Deal is a must-read for all Americans, especially the incoming administration and the new Congress. Jill Lawrence's in-depth interviews and deep knowledge about how Congress works bring to life the personalities, process and politics of tough but successful negotiations on the federal budget, the Veterans Administration, federal land swaps and the food stamp program. Lawrence, one of America's best congressional reporters, shows that Congress is still capable of breaking the policy gridlock and stifling polarization that plague our democracy—that

compromise, pragmatism and bipartisanship are not dead on Capitol Hill. Surprisingly, when party leaders make strategic choices to work together, Congress can get something done."

—James Thurber, founder of American University's Center for Congressional and Presidential Studies and co-author of *American Gridlock: The Sources, Character and Impact of Political Polarization*

"Highly recommended to anyone who wants to understand how Capitol Hill works. Legislating is as important for politicians to master as campaigning—arguably even more so. But the former gets precious little attention compared to the latter. Jill Lawrence's collection of case studies successfully helps to address this imbalance: It illustrates, in clearly written and often fascinating detail, how some of the best-known figures in Congress, such as Paul Ryan and Bernie Sanders, worked with a variety of lesser-known lawmakers to achieve the compromises that made the passage of important bills possible."

—Chuck McCutcheon, co-author of *The Almanac of American Politics (*2012 and 2014 editions) and *Dog Whistles, Walk-Backs and Washington Handshakes: Decoding the Jargon, Slang, and Bluster of American Political Speech*

CONTENTS

FOREWORD

By Norman Ornstein

Do a word game about Congress during the Obama administration—what one word comes to mind if I say "Congress"?—and the most common answers would be "gridlock," "obstruction," "partisan" and "tribal." Those characterizations are not inaccurate. Over a long period of time, going back at least to the George W. Bush era with Dennis Hastert as speaker of the House, Congress has been "the broken branch," as Tom Mann and I called it in the title of our 2006 book.

The Constitution's first branch of government has largely been a desert when it comes to the previous standard of bipartisan comity. Major legislative accomplishments were limited to two years of actions accomplished without minority votes, only due to swollen majorities linked to President Obama. But there have been some unnoticed oases of achievement done in the traditional way.

Jill Lawrence shows us four of these, each significant in its own right, each involving a different set of House and Senate lawmakers, each spanning a huge gulf in ideology between the key protagonists, each involving widely disparate personalities. It is hard to imagine more differences in background, personality and approach than Patty Murray, the Democratic senator from Washington state, and Paul Ryan, the Republican representative from Janesville, Wisconsin—unless one considers Vermont Senator Bernie Sanders, the fiery independent and self-described democratic socialist, and Jeff Miller, the arch-conservative Republican representative from Florida's Panhandle.

But Murray and Ryan forged a working relationship of trust and accommodation to resolve an impasse over the budget that was a classic example of compromise and give-and-take. Enough lawmakers of both parties and both houses understood the time pressure and the imperatives to act—and the consequences of inaction—to pull the compromise over the finish line.

Sanders, after navigating disagreements with his Senate colleague John McCain, then hit a buzzsaw with Miller. But after a lengthy series of potshots each took at the other, and a period of deep distrust, they found their sweet spot, also driven by the imperative to act on veterans' health issues amidst the major Department of Veterans Affairs scandal. They reached an important agreement that ameliorated the urgent problems, even if they were unable to solve the issues once and for all.

The other two cases Lawrence details, on the long-delayed farm bill and its impasse over food stamps, and a difficult public lands package that faced problems among both Democrats and Republicans, were different in some ways, but also shared key characteristics with the other cases. Each required pragmatic lawmakers looking to achieve progress, patience to let obstacles fall away, and leadership support that overcame some strident opposition. The farm bill was a special case, one that involved years of negotiations and setbacks, of chambers rejecting careful leadership-driven compromises crafted in a House committee known for its bipartisan cooperation, before reaching an agreement that could pass muster. The public lands case had the advantage of a number of retiring members who saw an opening to cement their legacies.

While there are obvious differences in how these four success stories played out, there are real commonalities about finding conditions ripe for accomplishment and finding lawmakers with the right skills and mindsets. Jill Lawrence has herself skillfully and masterfully shown us why and how deals, and legislative action, are still possible. These well written and lively case studies are valuable for those reasons—but also as a template as we face a new and quite unique set of challenges for a Congress itself wondering how it will operate in the era of a President Donald Trump.

Norman Ornstein is a resident scholar at the American Enterprise Institute and co-author of It's Even Worse Than It Looks: How the American Constitutional System Collided with the New Politics of Extremism *and* The Broken Branch: How Congress is Failing America and How to Get It Back on Track.

PREFACE

The United States is so sharply divided, and its governing institutions in such a constant struggle to function, that it's easy to be depressed about the state of this nation. Republican obstructionism was the hallmark of Barack Obama's eight-year tenure, culminating in the GOP-controlled Senate's nine-month refusal to consider his nominee to the Supreme Court.

Congress set record lows for popularity and productivity during the Obama years, and volatility plagued the Republican Party. The rise of the anti-compromise, anti-establishment Tea Party movement led to the ouster of House Majority Leader Eric Cantor in a 2014 primary and, in 2015, the resignation of House Speaker John Boehner.

And yet.

Every once in a while, a green shoot appeared—a sign that some lawmakers in some circumstances could transcend the polarization that was rending the nation and bringing its business to a near-halt. These shoots took the form of bipartisan agreements that used to be routine but in this acid environment merit special attention.

The idea of examining the art of the political deal was presented to me by the brilliant Elaine C. Kamarck, director of the Center for Effective Public Management at the Brookings Institution. She knew that the American Political Science Association was publishing research on political negotiations and she was intrigued when, at a conference, she heard Senator Patty Murray talk about how she and Representative Paul Ryan were able to nail a budget deal that had eluded others for years. Elaine also knew that while studies of business negotiations were common, studies of political negotiations were quite rare.

I jumped at the chance to explore that Murray-Ryan budget deal and to see if there were other potential case studies of bipartisan compromise achieved in a highly polarized period. And it turned out there were. In a discouraging historical moment, we had stumbled on an uplifting topic that we both felt warranted more notice.

Elaine deserves tremendous credit for this brainstorm, and I can't thank her enough for offering me the chance to write on such a constructive topic. I hope it inspires current and future negotiators to seize their opportunities and gives them some practical ideas on how to succeed. I am also appreciative of the latitude afforded by Elaine and Brookings in how I reported these case studies. They are based on research and interviews with many of those involved in the negotiations, particularly the congressional aides in both parties who knew their subjects cold and put in countless hours with no guarantee of results.

The many aides I interviewed, Democrats and Republicans alike, were generous with their insights, details and time. Their contributions bring these case studies to life and offer lessons applicable to any political negotiation. Their honesty and openness were possible largely because they could speak on background, and I am more grateful than I can say for their help. There were two dozen of them and I'd thank them each by name if I could. Anyone who reads these accounts will come away with more faith in our system and a new appreciation of the people—both lawmakers and staff— who work very hard to make things happen. —*J.L.*

INTRODUCTION

Party polarization and gridlock are facts of political life, and they certainly get their share of attention. But every once in a while, driven by urgent needs, imminent deadlines and determined people, a compromise is reached, passed by Congress and signed by the president. Some of these deals are widely publicized, but some are not.

What can we learn about political negotiating from these breakthroughs and the environment in which they were achieved? What are the circumstances found by the American Political Science Association to be conducive to success, and were they present in these negotiations?

These case studies, sponsored by the Center for Effective Public Management at the Brookings Institution, highlight important negotiations and who and what made them work. They provide an inside view of the political negotiation process and illuminate tools, techniques and conditions that are necessary to succeed. In times dominated by a second-term Democratic president, an upstart conservative populist Tea Party movement and ruthless Republican obstructionism, we learn what staff negotiators were thinking and saying as they haggled over details and painfully inched their way to success.

Donald Trump presented himself throughout the 2016 presidential campaign as the consummate negotiator and dealmaker. You need flexibility, he said, along with hugs, cajoling and some "tug and pull." Hillary Clinton, speaking to women at a June 2015 technology conference in Santa Clara, California, said one of her goals if she became president would be to create "a nice warm purple space" for compromise in Washington. She was a skeptic when Barack Obama advanced the same idea in 2008. But the case studies in this book show that progress is possible in any era, even one that's among the most partisan and unproductive in U.S. history.

These are counter-narratives—examples of four times when our elected officials and their aides defied failure. Each drills down into the motivations of the players as well as the tradeoffs the many parties made and how they felt about them. All of this is set into two larger contexts: the ideological divide that dominates U.S. politics and the conditions the American Political Science Association has identified as conducive to successful negotiations.

The four case studies offer a revealing, ground-level look at the deep-seated conflicts in our daily headlines: tax hikes versus entitlement cuts, the federal versus private role in health care, developers versus conservationists, the precarious balance between farming interests and food-stamp recipients.

The common themes of these breakthroughs were urgency and deadlines, the more the better. The Murray-Ryan budget deal capped years of failure and brinksmanship that culminated in a two-week government shutdown and record-low ratings for Congress. The veterans deal came amid a public outcry over long waits for medical appointments, with the added incentive of an approaching recess during which lawmakers did not want to have to explain a failure to help veterans. The farm-bill deal was passed after three years and many controversies, yet didn't look all that different from what was proposed in the first place. The public lands deal benefitted from heavy demand for both conservation and development after years of inaction.

These agreements did not always live up to their promise. Yet they were bright spots in a dark landscape—snapshots of professional politicians and staff doing their jobs well, for the good of the nation, against the odds. In that respect they present a template for future negotiators on how to achieve that rarity of our political era, a deal.

CASE STUDY ONE

A BUDGET AGREEMENT
THAT SHOCKED DOOMSAYERS

Senator Patty Murray and Representative Paul Ryan did not have relaxing holidays in 2013. When they weren't closeted in a room with each other, they were texting, emailing and talking on the phone. Halloween came, and Thanksgiving, and the frenetic run-up to Christmas. As Americans ate, shopped and trick-or-treated, Ryan and Murray soldiered on. Their mission: find a way to keep the government open and solvent for at least a year or two. Find a way to stop the recurring political showdowns that had cost the nation money, stability and respect. That they succeeded made them unusual in these polarized times, and provides a hopeful template for future negotiators.

Congress is rarely popular, but 2013 was a year for the record books. Its Gallup approval rating plummeted from 19 percent in September to 11 percent amid a federal government shutdown in October, to 9 percent in November, on its way to a rock-bottom 14 percent average for the year.

The disaffection was earned. The 16-day government shutdown, triggered by conservatives trying to block funding for the Affordable Care Act known as Obamacare, was the latest of a series of fiscal emergencies that had rattled the country and the world. Congress was taking most of the blame, polls showed, and Republicans in Congress were faring particularly badly.

The standoff took the country once again to the verge of a debt default. It finally ended with passage of a law to raise the debt limit and fund the government until mid-January 2014, only three months away. The law also set up budget talks between the Republican House and the Democratic Senate to come up with a longer-term agreement by that mid-January deadline. And this time, to the surprise of a jaded America, the struggles produced a deal—a two year compromise that restored $63 billion to defense and domestic programs over two years, reduced the federal deficit by $23 billion over 10 years, and offered temporary relief from self-induced crises.

On a visit home just after the agreement was announced, Republican Senator Johnny Isakson of Georgia found himself accosted by grateful citizens at church, at the mall, at the airport, even at a dinner party with GOP activists. They all had the same thing to say: Thank goodness you have finally gotten your act together. "I received not one negative comment," Isakson said on the Senate floor. The partisans naturally engaged in "some grumbling about not getting this or that," he said, but like everyone else he encountered, they were relieved that the string of threats and crises was over.

The respite would last only until September 30, 2015, and President Obama would reignite the old arguments months before that in a budget that proposed to lift caps on spending. It was, the administration said, a blueprint based on the expiring deal. Here is an analysis of how that deal came together, based on research and interviews with inside players from both parties.

A GULF APART

There had been little cause for optimism in late 2013, given the debacles of the preceding years. Among them were the August 2011 debt ceiling crisis, which brought the United States to the edge of default and was resolved with a Budget Control Act requiring $1.2 trillion in spending cuts across the board ("sequestration") early in 2013 unless a "super committee" produced a more rational distribution of resources; the failure of the super committee that November to agree on an alternate plan; the 2012 year-end "fiscal cliff," a combustible mix of expiring tax cuts, impending sequestration and the need to again raise the debt ceiling; and then, capping years of brinksmanship, the 2013 shutdown—"peak bleak," as *Slate*'s John Dickerson put it.

It took an autumn of extreme dysfunction and public-relations angst to bring about official talks on the wildly disparate House and Senate budgets. Murray went to the floor 21 times to urge such a conference but was rebuffed. In a June memo, Republicans said a House-Senate budget conference was premature and would complicate ongoing efforts to solve the debt crisis. "It seemed to be an exercise in futility," said a Republican familiar with both budgets. "The two sides were on different planets in a lot of ways."

This was the environment—charged, polarized, urgent—in which negotiations commenced between a pair of highly unlikely partners.

Ryan was and remains a symbolic North Star for small-government conservatives. At 45, he had spent more than a third of his life in the House and even longer than that in politics. Ryan grew up in Janesville, Wisconsin, where his grandfather founded a construction firm in the 1880s. He started working on campaigns during college, held a series of jobs on and around Capitol Hill, and won his House seat at age 28. As chairman of the House Budget Committee for four years starting in 2011, Ryan produced starkly conservative blueprints that cut taxes and popular programs. They regularly drew verbs like "eviscerate" and adjectives like "draconian" from liberals, and went nowhere in the Democratic Senate. But they made him a hero and thought leader among his fellow Republicans, and earned him the vice presidential slot on the GOP ticket in 2012.

A generation older than Ryan, Murray was part of the 1992 "year of the woman" when an unprecedented four women were elected to the Senate. She and her six siblings grew up in Bothell, Washington, where her father ran a five-and-dime store on Main Street. Back when her children were small, Murray visited the state capitol to protest plans to end their preschool program. Recalling the incident on the Senate floor in 2013, she said, "One legislator in particular told me I was just a mom in tennis shoes—and I had no chance of changing things." The soft-spoken, 5-foot teacher commandeered the phrase and used it in winning campaigns for school board, state Senate and U.S. Senate. At the time of her negotiations with Ryan, Murray was 63, the No. 4 Democratic leader in the Senate and one of Democratic Leader Harry Reid's closest advisers. She chaired the Senate Budget Committee in 2013 and 2014.

Murray and Ryan personally embodied the gulf between their parties. In 2013, the year of their partnership, Ryan earned a zero rating from the liberal Americans for Democratic Action and Murray earned the same from the American Conservative Union. People joked that the pair had a 5 percent chance of producing an agreement. "They couldn't believe I walked into a room with him," Murray said of her fellow Democrats as she sat beside Ryan for a post-deal interview with NBC's "Meet The Press."

On the House floor, Ryan had summed up the fraught state of play in one sentence: "We have been at each other's throats for a long time." Yet circumstances were converging to create a relatively hospitable environment for negotiations. At the end of the year, about when Ryan and Murray were announcing their deal, the American Political Science Association (APSA) published a 182-page report called *Negotiating Agreement in Politics* (now a Brookings Institution Press book called *Political Negotiation*). By choice and happenstance, the major ingredients the report deemed necessary for success were present in the Murray-Ryan process.

A DAUNTING OBSTACLE COURSE

The sequester was a fiscal straitjacket designed to be so intolerable to both parties that they would feel compelled to come up with a better way to spend and save money. The $1.2 trillion in cuts over 10 years were split between defense and non-defense discretionary spending. Lawmakers in both parties were upset that some $20 billion was about to be lopped off the Pentagon budget early in 2014—none more so than Murray, who represented 85,000 workers at Boeing and personnel at eight military bases in her state. Democrats were also concerned about automatic cuts in the areas of education, transportation, social services and research, particularly medical research.

The bottom lines for each party were familiar and not conducive to compromise. Adhering to the GOP catechism, Ryan ruled out all new taxes. In addition, he was determined to preserve deficit reduction, and not just by any means. He was committed to permanent, structural changes in automatic federal spending that would generate increasing savings over time. Democrats refused to consider such changes in Social Security or Medicare, thus taking the major mandatory spending programs off the table. They also insisted that any restoration of defense money be matched on the domestic side, a critical precedent in their view.

One further potential complication was the possibility that Ryan might retain national ambitions. Brokering a bipartisan budget agreement that necessarily gave Democrats some "wins" would not be a selling point in GOP primaries. Ryan announced in January 2015 that he was not going to run for president in 2016. It's not clear if he had made that decision by late 2013, but he and his party were ready at that point to accept two difficult realities: that Obama had been reelected, and that more conflict-driven paralysis would reflect badly on them and Congress. "Look, I was part of the last presidential election. We tried defeating this president. I wish we would have," Ryan said on the floor. "To really do what we think needs to be done, we are going to have to win some elections. And in the meantime, let's try and make this divided government work."

That it hadn't worked for so long was trying to many on Capitol Hill, especially those most directly involved in budget negotiations that had foundered. The failure of the super committee to come up with a plan to kill the sequester, especially its slashes to the Pentagon, was a major blow.

Some leading lawmakers spun the past failures—including 2011 negotiations led by Vice President Joe Biden and a bipartisan Senate "Gang of Six" that met the same year—as the foundation on which the eventual Murray-Ryan agreement was built. Murray was "walking into a minefield" as chair of the super committee, said Senator Dick Durbin, an Illinois Democrat. And while it did not succeed, Durbin said, "she learned in the process not only more about our budget challenge but also more about the leaders in the budget process. And I think it was that painful experience with the super committee that set the stage for the much more successful negotiation over this budget agreement with Paul Ryan."

South Carolina Representative James Clyburn, a Democrat on the House Budget Committee, noted on the House floor that he was on the super committee and "we didn't get much done." He also said he was part of the Biden Group "and we didn't get anything done." He added that "the third time seems to be the charm." Ryan told Clyburn that his time on "these prior endeavors" had not been wasted. "That was productive time because the findings of those groups were used in this agreement," he said.

PRIVATE PARTNERS AND THE IMPORTANCE OF TRUST

The work that came before was one element of many that made the third time the charm, as Clyburn put it. The crucial factor may have been that leaders in both parties wanted an agreement. That was especially true for Republicans. The shutdown had not been kind to them. In an October 2013 *Washington Post/ABC News* poll, 53 percent blamed the GOP for the shutdown (compared with 29 percent who blamed Obama), and a record low of 32 percent viewed the party favorably. The pressure was on House Speaker John Boehner to prove that the GOP could govern responsibly.

At the most basic level, to have a House-Senate conference on the budget, both chambers need to pass a budget. With Murray at the helm, the Senate in March 2013 had passed its first budget in four years. So that prerequisite was in place. Fortunately for the country, other necessary but less defined elements of a successful negotiation were also coming together.

Murray and Ryan had been meeting and talking from the time she was named chairman, starting with a get-to-know-you breakfast. Between then and the October start of official talks, the pair had steadily built up mutual trust. "Too often in politics, people use what they hear to go slam them later," Murray said at a *Fortune* Most Powerful Women event in March 2014. "We had to agree not to do that, but also know that that agreement was going to stay in place." The proof came as they held conversations over a period of months "and none wound up in the paper the next day," Ryan said in an email read aloud by Nina Easton, the *Fortune* moderator.

That trust gave them a head start when they found themselves tasked with forging a budget agreement in a matter of weeks. So did the things they learned about each other over those months of careful listening. "My goal was to find out what made him tick. What does he feel passionate about? He needed a story about what he won and I needed a story about what I won. Before I could do that I had to find out what was most important to him," Murray said.

The pair's personalities and some unexpected commonalities smoothed the way. They both had endured shattering experiences involving their fathers. Ryan's died suddenly of a heart attack when he was 16, and his family received Social Security survivor benefits. Murray's father was diagnosed with multiple sclerosis when she was 15. He had to stop working, and the strapped family relied on food stamps for a few months. On the lighter side, the two lawmakers shared affinities for football and fishing, and teased each other about both as a way of easing tensions.

"I fish and he fishes. I salmon fish. He fishes for some weird fish that they fish for [musky and walleye, according to Ryan's office]. We eat what I catch. We could kind of share stories about that,"

Murray said at the *Fortune* forum. She added that their football teams—the Seattle Seahawks and the Green Bay Packers—were "probably the thing that kept us laughing the most. ... His team got kicked out of the season early on because their quarterback was injured. I would just give Paul grief about this football team. And of course my team kept doing better and better. It was kind of the go-to laugh that we could share." When their agreement passed Congress, Murray said, she called the Seahawks and "our quarterback signed a jersey to Paul Ryan." She added: "Finding something in common with the other person, so you have a kind of a go-to when things get tough, is really important."

Privacy was another critical element of the negotiations. Murray and Ryan each had the confidence of their leaders to negotiate for their parties and make judgments about what would or wouldn't fly with their colleagues. Polarizing, high-profile players in earlier negotiations, including Obama, Reid and Boehner, stayed in the background—resulting in a welcome dearth of press attention.

Murray says long-distance communications also helped foster privacy. The chief negotiators spent a lot of time at home during their eight-week sprint to the finish—Ryan in Janesville, Wisconsin, and Murray in Whidbey Island, Washington. "Much of our negotiating was on the phone, talking to each other from our homes," Murray said. At one difficult moment, she looked out her window at the mountains and the water. "I remember thinking 'Thank God I'm not in Washington, D.C. I can just calm down right here.' I think he had to do the same thing."

When they were in Washington, talks were held in Murray's Senate hideaway, a small room decorated in neutral tones of cream and beige, in a neutral location off the Capitol Rotunda, about equidistant from the House and Senate chambers.

COLD HARD REALITIES

No scenic or soothing location could paper over the chasm between the Republican House budget and the Democratic Senate budget, and the clashing priorities they reflected. The conferees spent weeks airing their differences. "We've got that part down cold," Ryan said in mid-November. In Murray's undramatic hideaway, "they pushed and pushed and pushed," a Democratic aide recalled. Ryan pushed for structural changes to Medicare, Medicaid and the Affordable Care Act. Murray pushed to close corporate tax loopholes. "There was a long period of pushing things that in the end, neither could agree to," the aide said. "Those things always came back. Neither of them ever walked away or ended negotiations over it. Neither one, after getting told 'no' for the 15th time, walked away."

At the same time, however, the pair were looking for areas of agreement. "We knew that if we forced each other to compromise a core principle, we would get nowhere. That is why we decided to focus on where the common ground is," Ryan said. He described that as taking "all the different budgets that were offered" and laying them on top of each other to see where they overlapped—where both sides agreed there was waste, cronyism, corporate welfare or "auto-pilot mandatory spending" that could be reformed.

It wasn't quite that simple, of course.

One thing that helped was flexibility. The deal could be long or short, large or small. The negotiators decided to avoid a repeat of fruitless quests for "grand bargains" that addressed major issues and forced the parties, in the words of a Republican aide, to "give up what they care about, inflict pain, do violence to their principles." Nor did they attempt to reconcile their respective 10-year budgets. They also worked to avoid the frequent negotiating pitfall of one side using a low-priority item as a bargaining chip—as in "We'll only support this, which we don't really care about, if you support this other thing, which causes you pain."

Perhaps the most important decision was to limit the time frame. "The key was coming to an understanding of what the scope of the agreement would be," Chris Van Hollen of Maryland, a senator who was then the senior Democrat on the House Budget Committee, said in an interview. "You could have set the goal [as] let's find a way to deal with the sequester for a ten-year period, an eight-year period or a one-year period. At the end of the day it was a two-year period. That was partly dictated by how much in offsets was available. Where could you identify savings and revenue?"

MATH PROBLEMS

That was not a small question. Democrats would only approve a deal that restored domestic spending, and Republicans would only approve one that offset that spending with revenue so as not to increase the deficit. Democrats did not give Republicans the chance to tackle Medicare and Social Security—the main drivers of mandatory, automatic spending and prime candidates for the type of permanent structural changes at the top of Ryan's priority list.

Republicans not only refused to raise taxes, they also rebuffed Democrats on their attempts to end subsidies and tax breaks they viewed as corporate welfare. Their targets during the debate included oil companies, agribusinesses, private jet and yacht owners, and companies hiding profits overseas. "I'm disappointed we weren't able to close even a single corporate loophole," Murray said in announcing the package. Ryan said the negotiators did target cronyism and corporate welfare—and the Heritage Foundation, for instance, noted the end of a 2005 program under which the government helped oil and gas companies research new exploration and production technologies.

That's hardly comparable to the headliners Murray and her party were after, big-ticket loopholes that Ryan wanted to address as part of a broader tax reform drive that lowered corporate rates. But in the meantime, where were he and Murray going to find the revenue they needed to ease the sequester without blowing up the deficit? The answer was, in large part, fees. Their package added security fees to airline tickets; increased the fees businesses pay the government to insure their pensions; extended temporary user fees collected by customs and border agents; charged states for management of mineral leases on their land; and let the National Resources Conservation Service charge for helping develop conservation plans.

Among the most inflammatory elements of the emerging package were savings Ryan sought from the civil service and military pension systems. His budgets, in line with the bipartisan Simpson-Bowles deficit commission, had proposed saving $132 billion over 10 years by raising federal workers' pension contributions from .8 percent of salary to about 6.3 percent. In his talks with Murray, Ryan settled for a much lower yield of $20 billion over 10 years—the same savings as an Obama budget that would have increased federal worker pension contributions by 1.2 percentage points.

But even the $20 billion was a deal-breaker for some Democrats, who threatened to vote against the whole package on the floor— potentially killing it—if the provision wasn't changed. In negotiations that came down to the wire, Ryan and Murray agreed to raise the pension contribution to 4.4 percent, but only for new hires. The savings amounted to $6 billion over 10 years.

Republicans also proposed an even more contentious 1-percentage-point reduction in cost-of-living adjustments (COLAs) in pensions for working-age military retirees (those under 62). Ryan called it a modest change to a generous program. But it generated an uproar, especially because it applied to disabled veterans and survivors of fallen troops. Parades of senators and House members condemned it and promised to fix it quickly in follow-up legislation.

In announcing the deal in December 2013, Murray said the pensions posed a difficult challenge. "He's a tough negotiator in case any of you want to know," she said of Ryan. The pair explained their rationales for accepting the cuts, and they weren't the same. Ryan called it "only fair that hard-working taxpayers" who pay for the federal and military benefits "are treated fairly as well." Murray said that if she and Ryan hadn't reached a compromise, "many of these same people would be facing furloughs, layoffs and uncertainty."

TESTING THE FAITHFUL

The deficit reduction in the Murray-Ryan agreement had been backloaded to the point where more than half of it was now outside the original 10-year sequester window. Anti-tax, anti-spending and Tea Party groups were livid about that and many other aspects of the deal. Detractors included FreedomWorks, the Club for Growth (which penalized lawmakers for yes votes on Murray-Ryan in its annual scorecard), Heritage Action (which had helped incite the 2013 government shutdown over Obamacare), Senator Jeff Sessions of Alabama, the senior Republican on the Senate Budget Committee, and Senator Tom Coburn of Oklahoma, the chamber's self-appointed spending auditor.

"I feel like John the Baptist in the wilderness," Coburn said on the floor, but he forged ahead with demands to know why Ryan and Murray hadn't tried harder to save more money. "We spent $978,000 to study romance novels," he said, and $500 million on "brand-new crystal stemware for all the embassies throughout the world," and $34 million on an abandoned, never-used camp for troops in Afghanistan.

The Murray-Ryan deal passed the Senate 64-36, with only nine of 45 Republican senators voting yes. Ryan persuaded 169 House Republicans to support the agreement, versus only 62 who opposed it. It passed 332-94.

Both negotiators were able to declare limited ideological victories—Ryan by holding the line on taxes and adding even more deficit reduction; Murray by rolling back cuts in domestic spending while preserving the major entitlements untouched. But there were larger accomplishments as well. Both could take credit for keeping the country on a stable path toward economic growth. The nonpartisan Congressional Budget Office said the original sequester, had it gone forward in 2014, would have cost 800,000 jobs. So the backloaded deficit reduction that infuriated the outside groups made sense in the context of an economic recovery that still hadn't caught fire at that point.

The arguments and disruptions themselves turned out to be expensive in several ways. The Bipartisan Policy Center projected that the 2011 debt ceiling fiasco would cost nearly $19 billion over 10 years, mostly in higher borrowing costs. White House and independent economists estimated that the 2013 shutdown lowered the Gross Domestic Product by $12 billion to $24 billion in the fourth quarter and reduced the private sector by 120,000 jobs in the first two weeks of October. Murray and Ryan, for the length of their agreement, spared the country those costs as well as the costs of falling confidence in America's capacity for fiscal management—including bond rating downgrades. "Mathematically, it seems like a small deal," said an aide who worked on it. "Given what we've gone through, it seems pretty monumental."

There were a couple of postscripts, however. In January 2014, the month after Obama signed the agreement, Congress reversed the military-pensions COLA cut for disabled veterans and survivors. In February, it restored the full COLA to all current service members and veterans, while keeping the 1-point reduction for those signing up after January 1, 2014. The changes left a 10-year, $6 billion hole. Lawmakers filled it by extending a cap on Medicare payments to medical providers.

A TEXTBOOK NEGOTIATION

Had we all been able to follow the progress of Ryan and Murray with a copy of the American Political Science Association's negotiations report in hand, we might have foreseen their success. Their road to a deal turns out to have been a model of "deliberative negotiation," in which participants search for fair compromises. Among the elements:

• Nonpartisan fact-finding. Trying to head off the across-the-board cuts of the sequester was a numbers game. That meant a key role for the Congressional Budget Office, which assesses the fiscal impact of congressional proposals. CBO "scores" are sometimes wielded as weapons in political battles, but both parties generally trust and rely on its calculations. Budget aides say it was extremely helpful during the Murray-Ryan process.

• Repeated interactions. Party leaders, budget committee members and their staffs had had plenty of contact over several years of failed talks. Murray and Ryan had personally been in touch for months by the time the government shutdown ended and their official negotiations began. The pair's budget aides knew each other and worked smoothly together, according to both sides.

• Penalty defaults. Both sides need to fear the consequences of failure. In this case, there was a ready-made penalty default—the across-the-board sequester already in place. Republicans had the additional motivation of trying to undo the image damage wreaked by the shutdown and earlier crises.

• Privacy. Murray and Ryan had this in spades, for one overriding reason: Their leaders empowered them "to figure it out themselves, very, very privately," according to a Democratic aide familiar with the negotiations. It didn't hurt that they were nearly 2,000 miles apart at various points, communicating one-on-one without anyone else around.

The APSA report also discussed "integrative negotiation," in which many issues are on the table at once and parties trade away their low priorities in exchange for concessions on high-priority concerns. The Murray-Ryan process, which accepted that both sides needed wins and included many examples of give and take, also followed that pattern to some extent. But both Republicans and Democrats imposed very tight constraints. Neither party had to alter its most meaningful principles or programs. The top issues on each side remained unaddressed, leaving open the question of how a future negotiation on a grander scale would fare.

Still, at that Silicon Valley technology conference for women in 2015, Hillary Clinton singled out Murray and Ryan as a model for what she hoped would happen more often if she became president. "They actually talked to each other," she said, feigning shock. "They didn't show up at a big conference table, with phalanxes of true believers on each side of them, with notebooks filled with argumentation. They had breakfast together. They had lunch together. They'd sit and talk about what each of them wanted, knowing that they couldn't agree on giving each other everything, but how could they make enough decisions to reach a consensus? And they did. So it's possible."

THE LIMITS OF GIVE AND TAKE

Some Democrats could envision future budget deals after Murray-Ryan, but nothing major. "If there's a majority among Republicans who want to raise the defense cap, our view is, 'well we also have to invest in education, scientific research, and other strategic areas.' And so there would be room for another agreement where we increase defense and non-defense investments in tandem," Van Hollen said. "My guess is it would have to be very limited in scope, but it would be better than the status quo."

Murray went on to test her negotiating skills as the senior Democrat on the Senate Health, Education, Labor and Pensions Committee, which was charged with rewriting the contentious No Child Left Behind Act. Ryan, the new chairman of the House Ways and Means Committee, hoped to be even more severely tested in the choppy waters of tax reform. Together they teamed up on a bill to promote "evidence-based policymaking." It created a 15-member commission to study how best to expand the use of data to evaluate the effectiveness of federal programs and tax expenditures.

This arose from Ryan and Murray texting back and forth on Election Night 2014. The two of them said that "we should do something to show that Democrats and Republicans can work together, even after an election like this," a Democratic aide said. Ryan's original version focused on spending programs; at Murray's suggestion, they added spending through the tax code as well.

"Great to be back working w/ @PRyan on a step to help govt work better for families & communities. -PM" Murray tweeted November 20, with a link to her press release. Ryan retweeted the Murray tweet and several subsequent links to editorials and articles about the proposal, including praise from liberal columnist E.J. Dionne Jr., the center-left Urban Institute and the *Huffington Post*.

Ryan and Murray also continued to poke at each other about their football teams. "#TBT to when I gave @PRyan a signed @DangeRussWilson @Seahawks jersey. Care for a friendly wager on Sunday?" Murray tweeted a few days before the Seahawks faced off against the Packers for the American Football Conference championship. "Great #TBT @PattyMurray, but it will be all @packers on Sunday. I've got some WI Gouda and Gray's beer to back it up. You're on! #GoPackGo," Ryan retorted. To which Murray replied, "You're on, @PRyan. I'll bet some @ Rainier_Beer & cheese from @WSUPullman that the @packers can't handle the @Seahawks & the 12s -PM."

The teasing tweets came just a couple of hours after Ryan, in his capacity as the GOP's new tax-reform chief, killed off a tax-hike idea that had been gathering bipartisan support in the Senate as a way to keep money flowing for highways. "We won't pass the gas tax," he said flatly to reporters at a GOP retreat in Baltimore.

Like that football game, which sent the triumphant Seahawks to the Super Bowl, his remark was a reminder that sometimes it's impossible for both sides to win. But as Ryan and Murray demonstrated, every once in a while victory is achievable, even if every component is not a winner for your side.

Murray demonstrated that once again by negotiating a bipartisan rewrite of the federal education law with GOP Senator Lamar Alexander. Obama signed it in December 2015. A few months later, he also signed the Evidence-Based Policymaking Commission Act—creating "a bipartisan commission to make recommendations for how the federal government could better use data to improve programs and the tax code." It was the idea Murray and Ryan had tossed around in text messages on an election night nearly two years earlier.

CASE STUDY TWO

A VETERANS DEAL
IN THE CROSSHAIRS OF CRISIS

If anything in America is sacred, it's veterans. Yet in the summer of 2014 they almost became casualties of America's deep and persistent red-blue divide.

A veterans health care scandal that year had outraged the nation. Veterans across the country were waiting months on end for appointments, and the wait times were being hidden. Up to 40 veterans in Phoenix died while waiting. Hundreds never even got onto a list. And retaliation was the order of the day for those who tried to blow the whistle.

It speaks volumes about the stature and political punch of veterans that from the moment the long-gathering scandal broke into public view on April 9, it took Congress less than four months to send President Obama the Access, Choice and Accountability Act. That is a split-second by Capitol Hill standards.

Yet the happy ending came after two volatile rounds of negotiations—one featuring a pair of famously irascible senators, the other arguably the two oddest bedfellows in Congress. Improbably, the senator at the center of both of them was Bernie Sanders, the war-averse chairman of the Senate Veterans Affairs Committee, the self-proclaimed democratic socialist from the liberal haven of Vermont, and the 2016 Democratic presidential candidate who came very close to wresting the party nomination from Hillary Clinton.

Sanders grew up in Brooklyn, the son of a Polish immigrant father, and moved to Vermont in 1968 as part of what *The Almanac of American Politics* calls the "hippie migration." Gruff, direct, sometimes sarcastic and given to "raised decibels" on the floor, as one observer put it, Sanders is a tough critic of Wall Street and an unapologetic advocate for a "Medicare-for-all" single-payer health system. The former Burlington mayor and House member was elected to the Senate in 2006—not as a Democrat but as an independent. He has identified himself as a socialist for decades.

The first round of negotiations starred Sanders and Senator John McCain, the feisty Arizona Republican and Navy veteran who spent more than five years as a Vietnam prisoner of war. The GOP presidential nominee in 2008, McCain can be witty and charming but is also known for having a temper and holding grudges. The second pitted Sanders against Representative Jeff Miller, a small-government, low-taxes conservative from the religious, military-heavy north Florida panhandle.

And there you have it, the perfect set-up for a two-act sitcom. The only socialist in Congress gets locked in a room with a top Senate conservative and they can't come out until they agree on something. Then repeat with a top House conservative.

All the players, from Congress to the White House, agreed on two overarching goals: to assure that veterans received timely care and to give authorities at the Department of Veterans Affairs the tools they needed to fire problematic employees. Despite that clarity, however, the process was complicated.

Both the Sanders-McCain and Sanders-Miller negotiations were to a large extent a proxy for the two parties' epic, long-running battle over the size and role of the federal government and, in particular, its involvement in health care. Furthermore, some of the conditions the American Political Science Association (APSA) has identified as ideal for forging compromise were conspicuously absent. For a start, Sanders did not have personal relationships with McCain or Miller. Second, the negotiators were operating in a fast-moving crisis environment rife with opportunities for mistrust and misunderstanding. And third, the process was closely watched and occasionally explosive. At one point, the media reported that prospects for a deal had disintegrated.

But these negotiators set an example for future dealmakers in the way they kept at it, no matter what obstacles arose. Meeting deadlines, political pressure and a sense of duty prevailed in the end. Lawmakers were heading home for a five-week pre-election recess, and no one in either party wanted to tell constituents that they had failed to help veterans.

A SCANDAL ERUPTS

The need for help was not in doubt. The VA health system is the largest in the nation, with some 1,600 medical centers, community clinics and other facilities; 288,000 employees; a $55 billion medical care budget; and 236,000 appointments daily.

In recent years, the system has confronted the twin challenges of an aging veterans population and the toll of long wars in Afghanistan and Iraq. Some 2 million new veterans had enrolled in four years, Sanders said at a July 2014 news conference, most as a result of those two wars. Moreover, he said, half a million troops had returned from those wars with post-traumatic stress disorder or traumatic brain injury.

The strain on the system was coming to light in occasional cases of egregious failure. In one hair-raising example, Barry Coates, 44, told the House Veterans Affairs Committee that he was dying of cancer because VA personnel at several facilities in South Carolina diagnosed him with hemorrhoids for a year before doing a colonoscopy. By then he had Stage 4 cancer. "Due to the inadequate and lack of follow-up care I received through the VA system, I stand before you terminally ill today," he said as lawmakers became angry and even tearful.

Coates was the first witness at that hearing on April 9, 2014. His testimony and the responses to it were so dramatic that barely anyone noticed when, 90 minutes later, the Phoenix situation came up in public for the first time. Miller wanted to know if Dr. Thomas Lynch, the VA's assistant deputy undersecretary for health clinical operations, was aware that the VA system in Phoenix was using two lists to make it appear that veterans were waiting less than a month for appointments when in truth they were waiting far longer. "It appears there could be as many as 40 veterans whose deaths could be related to delays in care. Were you made aware of these unofficial lists in any part of your lookback?" Miller asked.

"No, I was not," Lynch replied.

"So your people had two lists and they even kept it from your knowledge. Does that make you even internally question the validity of the information being used in your lookback and your reviews?" Miller asked.

"At the moment it does not," Lynch replied.

At that point, Miller ordered all potential evidence in Phoenix to be preserved and asked the VA inspector general to investigate as soon as possible.

Across the country in Phoenix, Dennis Wagner set to work. For four months, the investigative reporter for *The Arizona Republic* had been interviewing whistleblowers and requesting documents under the Freedom of Information Act. As he watched Miller's exchange in an online webcast, he knew he had to publish immediately lest another media outlet beat him on his own story.

To his surprise, Wagner says, Miller's revelation and his own extensive, detailed article documenting the scandal were greeted with "the resounding sound of silence." For nearly two weeks nothing happened, except that Wagner was inundated with tips from VA whistleblowers all over the country.

Then, on April 23, CNN came out with its own version of the Phoenix story. And the dam broke.

It turned out that, nationwide, the VA was coping with the onslaught of need by delaying appointments and treatment, manipulating schedules, falsifying records and possibly engaging in fraud. Throughout May, Miller fired off one press release after another as reports of preventable deaths, whistleblower retaliation and attempted cover-ups, including destruction of documents, piled up.

On May 1, VA Secretary Eric Shinseki put three top Phoenix officials on administrative leave. On May 5, the American Legion called for Shinseki's resignation. On May 15, Shinseki delivered what Miller called an "out-of-touch performance" at a Senate hearing and Obama designated his deputy chief of staff, Rob Nabors, to manage the crisis. VA Undersecretary for Health Robert Petzel, another witness at that hearing, resigned the next day.

On May 28, an interim report from the VA inspector general found it was taking an average of 115 days for veterans in Phoenix to get primary care, as opposed to the 24 days shown on official records—and 1,700 people seeking appointments were not on any list at all. The IG called the Phoenix problems systemic and said he had opened investigations at 42 VA health centers.

That same night, at one of several primetime hearings on the House side, Miller accused the VA of withholding documents despite a weeks-old subpoena. "Veterans' health is at stake and I will not stand for a department cover-up," he said. Maine Representative Mike Michaud, the senior Democrat on the committee, said the situation had become "increasingly difficult and emotionally charged." He added: "We'll get to the bottom of this and uncover the truth." Two days later, after a meeting with Obama, Shinseki resigned.

The intensity level was high and stayed that way. In just one indicator, Miller held 14 hearings between May 28 and final passage of the veterans compromise in late July. His topics included treatment of whistleblowers, bonuses for senior VA officials, "bureaucratic barriers" to VA care, comparing VA practices to the private sector, how to give veterans private health-care choices, and how to restore trust. There was also one about access to mental health care. It was called "Service Should Not Lead to Suicide."

On June 9, the VA reported that 57,000 veterans at its facilities were waiting more than 90 days for an appointment and that another 64,000 were not on a waiting list although they had sought care. Miller responded that "corruption is ingrained" in the system. "The only way to rid the department of this widespread dishonesty and duplicity is to pull it out by the roots," he said. The next day the House passed a bill giving veterans better access to care by a unanimous 426-0 vote. It had already given new firing authority to VA officials on a 390-33 vote in May.

TWO SENATE SCRAPPERS

The Senate also acted quickly, but its process was pricklier, reflecting the personalities and priorities of the top negotiators. McCain was not on the Veterans Affairs Committee chaired by Sanders, but he was the senior Republican on the Armed Services Committee and a longtime leader on defense and veterans issues. On top of that, his state was ground zero for the scheduling crisis. In early June, he introduced a major bill embodying his party's response to the scandal and stepped up as Sanders' GOP negotiating partner.

McCain's bill put a new issue on the table—giving private-sector health care choices to veterans who lived far away from VA medical facilities. Sanders, who had been focused on fixing scheduling and strengthening the VA internally, learned of McCain's new idea when it showed up in McCain's bill. As one aide put it, "This was not an element of the initial crisis. Distance was not necessarily the problem that everyone had been talking about. This was adding a new dimension." Over in the House, Miller saw the McCain provision, liked it, and quickly added it to the fast-moving House bill.

Sanders and McCain, meanwhile, were living up to their

reputations as scrappers. They were arguing—or making their points forcefully, as a Sanders aide prefers to put it—practically until the moment they announced their deal, culminating in a last-minute clash over McCain's long-distance provision. It was not "a knockdown drag-out fight. A little heated? Yes. A lot heated? I wouldn't characterize it as that," said a person familiar with the incident. "I don't think they ever had a full breakdown. There were moments when folks needed to go off and think a little. But you never had that 'we're going to go to our corners for a week.' They both did their best to negotiate very quickly."

The roots of the problem lay in the ongoing polarization in Congress. As usual, the two sides were divided over conflicting core philosophies of government and wary and suspicious of the other side. "Sanders had the view that McCain was trying to take away the VA and that was his ultimate intention. McCain had the view that Sanders was always going to prop up the VA and never accept any criticism of it," says Ian DePlanque, chief lobbyist for the American Legion, the country's largest veterans organization.

Neither was truly the case, he says, but that was the impression the pair gave. McCain's statements were focused on choice and private care, DePlanque says, reflecting the Republican view that the private sector would almost always do better than the government. On the other side, he says, Sanders' statements suggested that "he wanted to use the VA as a model for what single-payer could look like across the country. He has had a tendency to want to show the best of it."

In reality, the pair were pragmatic if occasionally hotheaded negotiators. McCain did not want to get rid of the VA and Sanders did not believe the VA was perfect; in fact, he had called the Phoenix revelations "reprehensible" and "totally intolerable." He agreed to give veterans the choice of private care for both scheduling and distance reasons, and McCain agreed to limit the choice program to a two-year trial. Both agreed on expanded firing authority, and they compromised on how much due process to allow for those who were dismissed.

The pair included a number of other provisions, such as in-state tuition for all veterans and spouses of troops killed in the line of duty and more health services for sexual assault victims. They also set up reviews to evaluate capital planning, scheduling technology, and overall VA management and delivery of care. And they agreed to classify the whole bill as emergency spending, a cost of war. That meant it was exempt from the "pay as you go" rule that requires Congress to offset costs with cuts elsewhere.

When they went to the floor to announce their deal, McCain joked about the behind-the-scenes drama. "I respect the fact that Bernie Sanders is known as a fighter, and it's been a pleasure to do combat with him," he said with a laugh. Sanders said that "reaching a compromise among people who look at the world very differently is not easy," but that he and McCain had "tried our best."

Five days later, the Senate passed the Sanders-McCain bill 93-3. And then the real political fireworks started.

THE ODDEST BEDFELLOWS

Congress embodies American diversity in all its crazy glory, but Miller and Sanders had to set some kind of record for temperamental, cultural and ideological differences. Miller's Florida panhandle district is "culturally part of Dixie," his website says, and geographically so far west it is in the central time zone. The area is known as the Bible Belt, the Emerald Coast and, depending on who's doing the nicknaming, the Redneck Riviera or the American Riviera. Its economy is driven by agriculture, tourism and the military, including Eglin Air Force Base.

Miller's family first settled in Florida in the mid-1800s. His parents raised cattle and he started in politics as an aide to a Democratic state agriculture official. But he switched to the GOP in 1997 and won a state House seat a year later. When Representative Joe Scarborough left Congress in 2001 to become an MSNBC talk show host, Miller won the race to succeed him. *The Almanac of American Politics* called him "soft-spoken and a good listener" and a "forceful advocate" for cleaning up the VA. He tied with nine other House members as most conservative in a *National Journal* analysis of 2011 votes.

The strangeness of the Miller-Sanders pairing was "not lost on anybody involved in this negotiation," one Republican familiar with the discussions said wryly.

The staff aides who worked to reconcile the House and Senate bills had long-standing relationships, but aside from small talk about professional issues at a few joint hearings, Miller and Sanders did not. It wasn't like they could compare notes on their favorite football teams or fishing spots, as Democratic Senator Patty Murray and Republican Representative Paul Ryan had done during painstaking 2013 negotiations on a budget deal. Asked if the two veterans chairmen had anything in common, one aide replied, "No—aside from the goal that failure wasn't an option."

The first meeting of their negotiation was in the Senate dining room, and despite the gulf between them, it went smoothly. There were no awkward pauses. In fact, jokes flew across the breakfast table.

And at first it seemed their respective chambers were not all that far apart. Both the House and the Senate had passed two-year programs allowing veterans to use private care if they lived more than 40 miles from a VA hospital or clinic or were experiencing long waits for a primary-care appointment. Both required an independent evaluation of the Veterans Health Administration, which runs the VA's hospitals, clinics and other facilities. The House had previously passed separate bills on firing authority, in-state tuition for troops and surviving spouses, and authority for the VA to lease 26 new clinics and other facilities.

But there were differences—among them a number of Senate provisions that the House had not previously approved, such as the new services for sexual assault victims, directing that $500 million in leftover money be used to hire new VA medical staff, and emergency appropriations to finance the new private-care choice program. And there was a larger difference that suggested the road to compromise would not be smooth: Democrats, along with the disabled-veterans community, wanted to add new money to bolster the VA internally. Miller and the House leadership wanted to focus on the private-choice program.

The ideological gulf between the parties makes all Capitol Hill negotiations difficult, but this one had some special challenges. The two chairman were as far apart as politically possible on the right-to-left spectrum, and the backdrop to their negotiations was a residue of Democratic bitterness over George W. Bush's military and fiscal policies. The negotiators were also coping with a telescoped time period that didn't allow for much study of options; non-stop press coverage that magnified every step forward or back; pressures from leadership on both sides; and repeated instances of Republicans, Democrats or both feeling blindsided.

The nonpartisan Congressional Budget Office produced the first unpleasant shock with a cost projection just as both chambers were passing their bills. The CBO estimated that the Senate choice program would cost $35 billion in its first three years and ultimately rise to an astronomical $50 billion a year. The House program was even more expensive because it allowed private care if veterans couldn't get a VA appointment within two weeks, as opposed to a month in the Senate version.

The totals sent both sides scrambling to bring down their costs. There was nothing the negotiators could do about one cost driver, the CBO presumption that many more veterans would enroll in VA health care once the choice program kicked in. But on other issues, there was a quick meeting of the minds. The House agreed to a 30-day minimum wait to qualify for the choice program. The two sides decided that private insurance carried by veterans would be the primary coverage for private care that was not service-related, and that after the date of enactment, only combat veterans would be eligible for the choice program. A geodesic distance standard was applied. That is, to participate in the choice program, you had to live 40 miles from the nearest VA facility measured as the crow flies, or the shortest distance between two points. And that applied to any VA facility. If you lived within 40 miles of a VA dental clinic but needed radiation treatments, you were out of luck.

There was one issue big enough and controversial enough to sink the whole enterprise: whether the VA health system itself should get more money to fix its problems—and if so, how much and where to find it. The American Federation of Government Employees called understaffing at the VA "the number one cause of this crisis," and Sanders was a strong advocate of what he called strengthening VA capacities. From the start of the scandal, he had been asking for numbers from the VA—how many doctors it needed, how many facilities, how much money. At the same time, there were many concerns about VA management and spending decisions, among them that money was going unspent and private providers were seeing twice as many patients as those at the VA.

Miller was the lead skeptic. He talked of VA officials who had repeatedly assured Congress they had enough money to meet veterans' needs, and government watchdogs who were saying amid the scandal that they had no confidence in VA numbers. At one June hearing, Miller said Congress had allocated at least $2.4 billion in recent years to solve scheduling problems. "Why are we still using outdated scheduling software and programs?" he asked. Acting VA Inspector General Richard Griffin replied that "a lot of money has been wasted."

THINGS FALL APART

The whole process was nearly derailed when acting VA Secretary Sloan Gibson told senators at a July 16 hearing that the VA needed $17.6 billion to put itself right. The money would be used to hire more staff, upgrade technology, and build, lease and renovate facilities. Five days after the Gibson bombshell, Sanders, Gibson and staff experts gathered in Sanders' office. Miller, calling in from Florida, cross-examined Gibson about the basis for his request and was not happy with what he heard. "There wasn't a lot of detail behind these answers," said a person who was in the room. Miller "kept his cool" but "what we all heard was frustration."

Two days later, Miller held yet another hearing and had a chance to express himself directly to Gibson, one of the witnesses. Veterans are sacred but the VA is not, he told the acting VA chief, and "throwing billions into a system that has never been denied a dime will not automatically fix the perverse culture" there. Two days after that, the stolid chairman engaged in what for him qualified as a highly theatrical temper tantrum.

He stood on the House floor and held up what he said was a typical VA budget request from the Obama administration: "Over 1,300 pages in four volumes to justify the money that's spent at the Department of Veterans Affairs." Then he held up Gibson's request for $17.6 billion. "I have in recent days called it a three-page document," Miller said. "But actually, if you take the cover letter off, you take the closing page off, you have one page to justify $17.6 billion." He ripped off the pages as he spoke, held up the one page, and leveled his final salvo. "I actually believe that we could have already come to an agreement if Senator Sanders had not insisted on moving the goal posts and adding this $17.6 billion ask into a clearly defined conference committee."

Sanders himself had said in opening the July 16 hearing that "we have been making significant progress in the last month and I believe that we can reach an agreement very soon." But the Gibson request and the phone call with Miller marked a turning point. "From that point forward it was difficult," said an aide close to the negotiations. "From that point forward it seemed like there was a huge difference in opinion. Part of the problem was that they weren't in fact talking."

Republicans felt it was out of bounds to interject such a huge sum into the negotiation at such a late stage. They were also annoyed by floor speeches by Senate Majority Leader Harry Reid of Nevada. On June 2, Reid said Republicans had blocked a Sanders bill to help the VA meet veterans' needs back in February because they were worried about "busting the budget." He said they didn't worry about that when they sent hundreds of thousands of troops to Iraq on "the credit card of the taxpayers of America" and ran up a $1.5 trillion debt on that war alone. "Republicans ignore the true cost of democracy," Reid charged. "Republicans focus on the monetary costs only, the dollar bills, because any money going to our veterans is $1 less going to billionaires, corporations and unnecessary tax cuts."

On July 21, the same day as the phone call that so perturbed Miller, Reid was back on the floor. "We have spent trillions of dollars in two wars—unpaid for, by the way. That is what President Bush wanted, and that is what he got. He squandered the surplus we had—a surplus of over 10 years when he took office that was trillions of dollars," Reid said. "But now we are being asked to spend a few dollars to take care of these people who have come back in need—as our veterans," he said, and "it looks to me" as if the conference committee will fail. "Why? Because they have to spend money on these people on whom they were glad to spend money to take them to war. But now they are back. They are missing limbs. They have many post-traumatic stress problems, a lot of medical issues, and no money is there."

Sanders was "working to get to a place of yes," as one aide put it, but at the same time Republicans felt like Reid was beating them up. From the standpoint of GOP lawmakers, they had proven with passage of the private-choice bill and the earlier bills on tuition and new facilities that they were not pinching pennies. Now they were out to prove they could compromise. According to a person close to the negotiations, they were planning to do it by asking House and Senate conferees to vote July 24 on a "serious proposal" that included all the Senate provisions that were not in the stripped-down House bill. The idea was, "We'll show you we want a deal. We'll take every single one of these provisions. We were basically conceding. They could have known that if they had shown up and listened to what the offer was."

The offer, however, did not include any money at all toward Gibson's $17.6 billion request, which had arrived weeks after the House and Senate passed the bills the negotiators were trying to reconcile. Sanders and other Democrats were predictably livid. Mainly they resented what they viewed as Miller's high-handedness. He and Sanders were co-chairs of the conference committee, yet Miller had called a meeting without talking to Sanders about a time or even if it was constructive at that point to bring members together.

Instead of going to Miller's meeting, the aggrieved Senate Democrats held a press conference to vent about money and collegiality. Sanders responded to Miller's moving-the-goal-posts charge by saying he did move them—"to a much lower and more realistic number," $10 billion less than the initial Senate bill. He said he had tried to meet the Republicans "more than halfway" but was sad to conclude that "the good faith we have shown was not reciprocated by the other side." Miller's approach, he said, amounted to saying "come to a meeting, vote for my bill, end of discussion." He added: "That is not democracy."

Montana Senator Jon Tester, head of the Democrats' Senate campaign committee, then picked up where Reid had left off. "I was not here in 2003. But I would be willing to bet anybody that's here that they did not talk about offsetting the wars in Iraq when they decided to go in and fight that war. Taking care of our veterans is a cost of war," he said. "We need to depoliticize this and do right by our veterans. The fact is it's going to cost some money."

House Speaker John Boehner blamed the impasse on … Obama. "Bipartisan, bicameral negotiations were making good progress, until the White House began demanding more money with no accountability, and no strings attached. Now, I want to be clear: there's going to be no blank check for the president and his allies," Boehner said. Other Republicans blamed Sanders, who had invited

Gibson to assess VA's internal needs and ended up with what one aide called "a half-baked proposal" that arrived smack in the middle of a negotiation.

With the clock ticking toward a five-week recess starting August 4, the parties had fallen into their usual roles and stereotypes: Democrats focused on strengthening a frayed safety net, Republicans fretting about spending—in this case not just the amount but also the very real prospect of throwing good money after bad. The media reported that tensions had erupted into the open, negotiations had broken down and failure was imminent. "How VA Reform Fell Apart In Less Than 4 Days," said the *Huffington Post* headline.

But while Sanders and Miller were not talking, their aides continued to talk. They were still trying to think of new ways to pay for things, still trying to find ways to bridge the fiscal gap.

THE BREAKTHROUGH

John McCain often jokes that it's darkest before it gets totally black. But in an echo of the clash he had with Sanders just before they reached an agreement, the Miller-Sanders implosion also proved to be momentary—the last cathartic paroxysm before a compromise was reached just a couple of days later.

"There was a brief moment when each side was questioning the intentions and the motives of the other," said a Republican familiar with the negotiations. But both sides quickly realized that "we cannot go home in August without a deal because that would be a colossal failure of our responsibility first and foremost, but it would also be a political disaster."

The House had offered zero money for VA improvements, while Sanders had asked for close to $9 billion. In the end, both sides agreed to $5 billion. Another $1.5 billion went for leases of 27 major medical facilities in 18 states and Puerto Rico. The two sides also decided to create a Veterans Choice Fund and settled on putting $10 billion into it.

The new fund led to one of the stickiest disputes of the negotiation. The House wanted no time limits, so that Congress could replenish the fund and extend the program at any point without having to evaluate and renew it. Sanders wanted a time limit precisely so the program would be subject to evaluation and renewal.

The two sides ultimately agreed on a limit of three years—one more than the Senate had passed—or whenever the money ran out. The House had pressed for the extra year. The thinking was that the program would be more entrenched and there would be more evidence available on how it was working.

The final product also allowed the GOP to finesse the politics of paying for it. The House went along with the Senate's emergency spending designation, with a twist. Negotiators had earlier found $5 billion in savings to offset what they knew would be an expensive bill. Initially those savings were meant to defray the cost of the choice program. Now they were described as paying for the internal VA staffing and facilities upgrades—the part of the bill that was "least popular with conservatives," as one negotiator explained.

Accountability—whether to allow any due process to those being dismissed or demoted, a top priority of unions representing VA employees and executives—was one of the last issues to be settled and also one of the easiest. The House, which had offered no due process, agreed quickly to an appeal within a week, a decision within a month and no pay for the duration of the appeal. And true to its word, the House accepted almost all aspects of the broader Senate bill in exact or slightly modified form. The phrase "adopts the Senate provision" appears 22 times in a summary of the compromise bill.

At a press conference announcing the agreement, Sanders said getting to that point had been very difficult, due in part to "a lot of partisanship going on." He said the deal would not have happened without Miller's "determination and hard work." For his part, Miller called Sanders his good friend and said the volatility of the process had been exaggerated by the media. Asked if conservatives would support a bill with such a hefty price tag, Miller replied, "Taking care of our veterans is not an inexpensive proposition and our members understand this."

In the end both votes were close to unanimous—420-5 in the House, 91-3 in the Senate. Obama signed the VA bill August 7 at Fort Belvoir. The new law, he said, "will help us ensure that veterans have access to the care that they've earned."

A DIFFERENT KIND OF DEALMAKING

So how close did Miller and Sanders come to the ideal negotiation?

Some aspects of their collaboration matched the conditions APSA found to be harbingers of success. One was their reliance on nonpartisan fact-finders.

They weighed testimony and findings from victims, whistleblowers, inspectors and investigators from both inside and outside the VA. And though they were skeptical of the CBO cost projections, they took them into account in their deliberations.

The two men did not have a pre-existing relationship, a pattern of interaction or much of anything in common—elements that have been key in other deals, such as the Murray-Ryan budget agreement of 2013. However, some Sanders and Miller aides had worked together on veterans issues for as long as 15 years. That was crucial to continuous communication, especially when communication broke down among the principals.

Privacy, another key to the Murray-Ryan deal, was not a hallmark of this negotiation. The media glare was relentless, driven in part by Miller's constant hearings that showcased VA problems, failures and tragedies. The attention gave the ups and downs of the negotiations perhaps more dramatic import than they deserved, but at other times it was helpful in keeping up the pressure for a final deal.

Party VIPs were also in the mix, for better or worse. House GOP leaders provided big-picture guidance on what was doable but left the details to Miller and his staff. Reid went off on his own messaging tangent and that was not helpful, but it was not fatal either. In part that was because veterans issues have a unique ability to unite conservatives and liberals in the cause of helping those who served. The nation's obligations to its veterans were what mattered in the end.

The negotiators also had a major "penalty default," the term APSA uses for the idea that both sides must fear and dread the consequences of failure. The nation was riveted by the veterans scandal. People would have been disgusted had Congress done nothing to fix mistreatment of millions of heroes. And there was a hard deadline for avoiding such embarrassment, since lawmakers were headed home to campaign for re-election in early August.

In April 2015, the one-year anniversary of Miller's first public mention of the Phoenix scandal, a person involved in the negotiations looked back on the speed of the process and got a case of nerves. The private-choice program was completely new and, according to the experts at CBO, was going to be very expensive. In the typical congressional time frame for a new proposal, experts would have talked through the options at a series of hearings and offered suggestions on which would be most effective. "It was quick and there was a lot of pressure," this person said. "Where we are now, we're working out some of the kinks."

UNFINISHED BUSINESS

Even accounting for a very slow phase-in of the choice program, the CBO estimates proved wildly overblown. Nine months after enactment, only a half-billion dollars had been spent. On Capitol Hill, there was talk of changing the 40-mile minimum to use private care, now applying to distance from any VA facility, to distance from a VA facility that offered the type of care needed by the veteran. On its own, the VA had already added flexibility to the requirement that mileage be calculated as the crow flies.

A year after the scandal was revealed to the public at his committee hearing, Miller noted that not a single VA employee had been fired over wait times. "VA's chief problem—a widespread lack of accountability among failed employees—is as prevalent today as it was a year ago," he said.

For several months Miller considered a race for the Florida Senate seat expected to open up in 2016 as a result of Marco Rubio's run for the Republican presidential nomination. He eventually decided against making the race and in March 2016 announced he would retire from Congress altogether. President Donald Trump considered him as a potential secretary of the Department of Veterans Affairs, but in the end gave the job to the department's undersecretary for health, Dr. David Shulkin.

As for Sanders, a year after the veterans scandal revelation and his launch into an unlikely role as a practical bipartisan negotiator, he announced that he was running for the 2016 Democratic presidential nomination. In those remarks outside the Capitol, Sanders summoned veterans in an argument against the Supreme Court's *Citizens United* decision allowing individuals to contribute as much as they want to campaigns. "I'm the former chairman of the Senate Veterans Committee," he said that day. "And I can tell you I don't believe that the men and women who defended American democracy fought to create a situation where billionaires own the political process."

While Sanders had negotiated a deal that introduced private care into the VA system, a pillar of his campaign platform was government-run, single-payer health care for all. Railing against economic inequality and calling for "revolution," he energized young people and many other liberals, and shocked many Democrats by nearly derailing Hillary Clinton.

DePlanque had been promoted from deputy legislative director to legislative director for the American Legion. His assessment of progress was measured. Asked about conditions in the VA health system, he replied: "Better than they were? Yes. Fixed? No." If anything, that was overly optimistic.

By April 2015, Dennis Wagner and *The Arizona Republic* had won three major investigative journalism awards for their work uncovering the VA scandal. In October 2016, after a reporting odyssey that took him to seven VA hospitals across America, Wagner wrote that he had encountered "patchworks of success and failure, hope and despair. All in a churn of politics."

It was, he suggested, impossible to be definitive about the impact of the events of 2014. "Whatever good has been borne of scandal seems obscure in the dizzy vortex of denial, data, acronyms and partisanship," Wagner wrote. "What's clear is there's no panacea. Just a day-by-day process."

CASE STUDY THREE

A PUBLIC LANDS PUZZLE
WITH HUNDREDS OF PIECES

The federal government owns more than half the land in the West, and that makes Congress its real-estate agent. If you want to mine, drill, graze, log or build on federal land, you have to ask Congress. Likewise if you want to add new wilderness areas, parks, or wild and scenic rivers.

Clashes have always been inevitable, given the competing priorities of conservatives and liberals, developers and environmentalists, Westerners, Indian tribes and many other interests. But the atmosphere grew particularly fraught during President Obama's tenure. Two statistics tell the story: For five years, from March 2009 to March 2014, Congress did not add a single new wilderness area. And that stretch included the entire 112th Congress of 2011-2012, marking the first time a Congress had not created a wilderness area since passage of the Wilderness Act in 1964.

A convergence of pent-up demand, urgent deadlines and personnel shuffles on Capitol Hill created a window for discussions in 2014. But this was never going to be a simple process of putting a couple of lawmakers in a room and directing them to hash it out. Hundreds of bills had piled up during the five years of inaction. Scores of senators and representatives wanted them passed, or in some cases blocked, in states and districts all over the country.

The challenges ranged from choosing what to include, to Republican anger that had festered over the five-year period, to a Congress divided between GOP and Democratic control. The division meant that GOP and Democratic demands were pitted against each other and that all "four corners" of the Hill—House Republicans, House Democrats, Senate Democrats and Senate Republicans—needed to be part of the process. Months of talks commenced among a circle of aides who knew their bosses and their subject matter well, and who patiently jiggered and rejiggered dozens of moving parts.

"It was one of the smaller packages I ever worked on, and by far the most difficult," said a Democratic aide involved in the horse-trading.

In the end, 169 pages of energy and public-lands provisions were tucked into a must-pass defense bill as 2014 drew to a close. It was like Christmas morning for conservationists and developers alike—except that in many cases they had to accept lumps of coal along with their gifts.

The package created nearly 250,000 acres of wilderness in Colorado, Montana, Nevada, New Mexico and Washington state, and protected about 140 miles of rivers. It added or expanded more than a dozen national parks and put mineral development off limits on hundreds of thousands of acres of federal land. But it also streamlined permits for grazing and oil and gas drilling on federal land and opened 110,000 acres of federal land for economic and commercial use—including logging in part of Alaska's Tongass National Forest and mining in Arizona, Montana and Nevada.

This was not one of those heralded mega-deals announced by proud lawmakers at a triumphant press conference. It was a collection of mini-deals affecting people and places in 36 states in myriad different ways. One example, cited by Alaska Senator Lisa Murkowski to illustrate the minute real-estate transactions that require an act of Congress, was the conveyance of one acre of federal land to a school district in Minnesota. The overall package, she said on the floor, is "fair and balanced, bipartisan, bicameral, revenue-neutral—which is exceptionally important—and also addresses the need for conservation on one end and economic development and jobs and prosperity on the other end."

After all that time, what made it work? A classic mix of the circumstances determined by the American Political Science Association to be conducive to negotiations, starting with multiple deadlines. The political dynamic was changing due to a wave of retirements and the approach of midterm elections that seemed likely to put the Senate in Republican hands. Senior members of Congress with long-gestating projects saw the moment as an opportunity to achieve their own goals and those of their colleagues.

The aides doing the negotiating had to trust that they all sincerely wanted a deal and would not wreck its chances by spilling details outside their tight circle. Privacy and a relative dearth of press attention helped them keep outside pleaders to a minimum and maintain a rough balance between the demands of competing regional, economic and ideological factions.

Fortunately for the lead lawmakers and their aides at the table, as they were closing the deal in late 2014 most of Washington was consumed by a frenzied push for a $1.1 trillion "CRomnibus" funding bill to keep the government open for the next nine months. "I kept expecting it to get out there in a big way," a Democratic aide said of the lands package. But it flew largely under the radar until it was a *fait accompli*.

AN INAUSPICIOUS HISTORY

Years of tensions preceded the breakthrough moment, starting in 2006. Democrats held a narrow Senate majority and that year, after 12 years in the House minority, they won back a majority. Now running both chambers, they passed a modest public-lands bill in 2008—the last year of George W. Bush's presidency. A second, larger bill was planned, but Democrats ran out of time.

That turned out to be more of an opportunity for them than a problem. When they came back in early 2009, they not only continued to control the House and the Senate, they had won the White House and a 60-vote, filibuster-proof Senate majority. The newly empowered Senate Democrats promptly grafted a huge environmental package onto a five-page House bill to protect battlefields and other significant sites from the Revolutionary War and the War of 1812.

The result was a 466-page grab bag of some 160 individual bills. It designated more than 2 million acres of wilderness and more than 1,000 miles of wild and scenic rivers, putting the land and water off limits for development. Obama, signing the new law barely two months after his inauguration, described it as "among the most important in decades to protect, preserve, and pass down our nation's most treasured landscapes to future generations."

He called it bipartisan, and half of the 40 Republican senators did vote for it. But only 39 of 179 House members followed suit—not surprising in that they were asked to approve a sweeping Senate bill with an environmental tilt after one hour of floor debate, with no amendments allowed. "It was by fiat and dictate. They essentially assumed these people [Republicans] have no power," said a Republican staffer involved in land issues. "So they assembled a package of their own. They did what they wanted."

Going full steam ahead was a no-brainer from the Democratic perspective. "Of course there was no incentive to negotiate that package with Republicans," said a Democratic aide who helped put it together. "We didn't need to, so why would we? Republicans may feel resentment about that, but I don't think anybody could be surprised."

Democrats lost their filibuster-proof majority early in 2010 and Republicans swept to a House majority that fall. So the GOP was positioned to work its own will—or at least block Democrats' will—by early 2011. There would be no new parks or wilderness areas unless they addressed the rights of property owners and communities with plans to do more with the land than preserve it. And there would be no huge packages that took months or years to assemble. "We were not going to designate miles of wilderness and wild and scenic rivers," said one GOP aide familiar with the party mindset. "We weren't going to allow ... small land adjustment bills, that had a lot of support, to be held hostage for these big giant wilderness bills."

Senate Democrats kept having hearings and churning out public-lands bills. Republicans did the same in their own fashion. And very little of anything went anywhere. Washington Representative Doc Hastings, the new chairman of the House Natural Resources Committee, had a long history of fighting regulations and restrictions that he viewed as hampering economic development. He considered wilderness areas a one-way street in the wrong direction. Democrats, meanwhile, were focused on protection and didn't like the GOP emphasis on commercial use and property-owner rights.

The mantra for two Congresses in a row had been no package larger than 10 bills, according to a Democratic aide involved in land issues. But given that the bills typically affected only one location each, 10 weren't enough to provide ideological balance or the yes votes needed to pass. "The larger the package, the more states and districts it hits, the more likely you are to be successful," another Democrat said. Hundreds of bills piled up during the long pause on land and energy bills.

A WINDOW OPENS

The first hint that a thaw might be in the offing came in February 2014 when Hastings announced that he was going to retire. He had a bucket list topped by a Manhattan Project National Historical Park with locations in Oak Ridge, Tennessee; Los Alamos, New Mexico; and Hanford, Washington. Murkowski, the senior Republican on the Energy panel, also had a special project—a land deal called Sealaska that she had been working on for seven years. "You had Doc Hastings really rolling up his sleeves in the House and Senator Murkowski ... saying let's take this opportunity and run with it," said a Republican negotiator.

You also had a Senate majority leader, Harry Reid, who had his own near-and-dear lands priorities and recognized an opening for a deal when he saw it; a new chairman of the Senate Energy and Natural Resources Committee, Mary Landrieu of Louisiana, who was more conservative than many of her fellow Democrats and more sympathetic to development; and GOP Representative Rob Bishop, the chairman of the House public lands subcommittee, a practical-minded former Utah House speaker who saw wilderness as currency that could be used to secure items on the conservative wish list. Combining wilderness bills with multiple-use and "pro-energy" proposals, "that's a win-win. The wilderness bills that we may not love, at least we're getting something for them," said Fred Ferguson, a former Bishop aide who was involved in the negotiations.

Two developments in March of 2014 indicated the arrival of "an opportunity for a natural give and take," as a Republican central to the negotiations put it.

First, a new wilderness area managed to make it past Hastings and the rest of the congressional obstacle course. Sleeping Bear Dunes in Michigan beat the odds for a number of reasons. It had strong support from local citizens and from Republican Representative Dan Benishek and Democratic Senator Carl Levin. Also, it was what one Republican described as "a baby step." It created a wilderness inside an existing national seashore, so the impact of the wilderness designation would be relatively minimal.

In that sense it was a good bill to ease Republicans into a different frame of mind. For two Congresses, they had been highly successful at preventing new wilderness areas, and that was their default position. With Sleeping Bear Dunes, "They realized not all wilderness is bad, it's not all going to lock up land," a Republican aide recalled. "It became 'OK, let me give a little.'"

Like Hastings, Levin was retiring and trying to nail down his legacy. Nor did it hurt the prospects of Sleeping Bear Dunes that Levin was chairman of the Armed Services Committee and thus in charge of the Senate version of the National Defense Authorization Act (NDAA), the vehicle Hastings wanted to use for his Manhattan Project park and most likely the vehicle for a larger deal. "For sure we knew we would need him," a Republican aide said of Levin, "but that wasn't sole driver at the time."

The second development was that Hastings put the new Manhattan Project park about the atomic bomb into the 2014 NDAA. A natural fit with the defense bill, he had included it the year before but it didn't survive. This time, with his retirement imminent, Democrats seized on the opening. If Hastings was going to get his Manhattan Project park on the NDAA, the Senate Democratic majority reasoned, other members should have similar opportunities.

From the Democratic perspective, Republicans had reached a tipping point. "At some point somebody has to decide, 'Let's do it the old-fashioned way, which is 'one thing I hate for one thing I love,'" said a Democrat involved in the negotiations. "The absolute key was that Hastings was retiring."

While Republicans don't go that far, some acknowledge that Hastings was in a different position—"no longer constrained by the larger debate that we were all immersed in," as one put it. "You had somebody who could now be a little bit more parochial than he could be as chairman of the committee for the long haul. It gives you an opportunity to promote your own state interests a little bit more."

The Defense Precedent

The idea of using the defense authorization bill as a vehicle to create parks, protect wilderness and manage public lands is not as strange as it sounds. The military uses federal land for training, for instance, so the Pentagon is accustomed to dealing with agencies like the Bureau of Land Management and the U.S. Forest Service. The overlapping jurisdictions mean it's not unusual for natural-resources provisions to end up in the NDAA.

In this case, with the Manhattan Project park and a few other museums and memorials in the House bill, there was already a hook on which to hang a bigger package. Once each side believed the other was serious about a negotiation, their first task was to set criteria for what to include. Some 500 relevant bills had been introduced. One negotiator described the opening challenge this way: "What's the defensible circle that you can draw around one subset of those 500 bills, that you can then explain to people why they're outside it? You have to have a defensible metric."

The negotiators started with bills that had passed either the House or the Senate, and then added bills that had gone through the hearing and mark-up process in either chamber and were reported favorably to the floor. That was a contrast with the past, one Republican noted pointedly: "In 2009, things that had never seen the light of day suddenly appeared—50 things."

Another bruising 2009 memory was the inclusion of projects opposed by the House member representing the district. Democrats counter that the projects were supported by senators representing the same people. Still, the 2014 bill avoided the in-your-face approach. House members had their say.

That gave Hastings and other Republicans a good case to make to resisters. "People still had reflexive opposition" dating from 2009, said a GOP negotiator. "We told them 2009 was done to House Republicans over their objections. In 2014, they were a party to it. It was done for our members."

Broad acceptance across both chambers and parties was an existential necessity. The NDAA was one of the rare legislative trains leaving the station and, at that late stage of the 113th Congress, one of the last ones as well. Levin and Representative Howard "Buck" McKeon, his counterpart at the helm of the House Armed Services Committee, were willing to tack the lands package onto the NDAA—but only if they could be sure it would slide through without incident. If anyone was going to raise hell about anything in it, the package would be kicked to the curb.

Discussions entered an intensive phase in early fall. One Democrat described it in unvarnished terms: "Here's a list of what we have to have. Here's a list of the ones we really, really hate. Here's a list of 'if you put this language on page 4 we could swallow it.' And then you work that list."

The have-to-haves started with the Manhattan Project park, pushed by lawmakers in three states but first and foremost by Hastings, who was critical to any larger deal. Other must-do items included the transfer of lands for logging to the tribal-owned Sealaska Corp., a condition of doing business for Murkowski (the senior Republican on the Senate Energy and Natural Resources Committee and, after the midterms, its incoming chairman); a land swap that paved the way for mining by Resolution Copper, of prime importance to Arizona Senator John McCain (senior Republican on the Senate Armed Services Committee and its incoming chairman); and several Nevada projects sought by Reid (who would be demoted to minority leader in January 2015 and announce his 2016 retirement two months later).

Scores of other lawmakers also had dogs of various sizes and significance in the fight, from the Blackstone River Valley National Historical Park in tiny Rhode Island ("the birthplace of the American Industrial Revolution") to an expanded Alpine Lakes Wilderness in Washington state. Senator Richard Burr wanted to let people drive off-road vehicles on the beach at the Cape Hatteras National Seashore. Senator Jeff Bingaman wanted to turn Valles Caldera National Preserve into a national park. Hastings wanted to require road access to the top of Rattlesnake Mountain. All of these items had been pre-negotiated, some over the course of many years.

TRADEOFFS ON ALL SIDES

Given the polarized politics of 2014, even small items could be annoying or painful. For instance, House Republicans agreed to the First State National Park in Delaware and a Harriet Tubman National Historical Park with locations in Maryland and New York, even though Obama had already used the Antiquities Act to declare parts of them national monuments. Republicans had been highly critical of what they viewed as Obama's overuse of executive powers and now, with local citizens and their members of Congress seeking an upgrade to the more prestigious park designation, they were being asked to fix something "he did by dictate," a GOP staffer explained. "From a philosophical standpoint, if you don't believe the president should be out there willy-nilly signing paper to create a monument, are you encouraging him to make more of them if you convert it to a park?"

On the other hand, these were discrete, narrow parks in the East—not parks in the West that would lock up large areas of land. And the politics lined up. The Tubman park was in districts represented by a New York Democrat and a Maryland Republican, and they both wanted it. As for Delaware, its two senators and single House member were all Democrats, so there would be no GOP objections.

Democrats and environmentalists were also making concessions, some much more far-reaching than a town or tribe that wanted to mine or open a road. For instance, the NDAA included a Republican-sponsored "Grazing Improvement Act" that streamlined the permitting process and kept permits in place during lawsuits filed by environmental groups. It affected more than 22,000 ranchers in a dozen Western states. A bipartisan provision with similarly broad reach streamlined the permit process for oil and gas drilling on federal land.

The potential to bring the 2014 talks to a crashing halt lay with seemingly narrower items on the list, none more sensitive than Sealaska and Resolution Copper.

Murkowski had been negotiating for years on Sealaska, the Alaska Native regional corporation for Southeast Alaska, to finalize the transfer of land owed to tribes under the 1971 Alaska Native Claims Settlement Act. The compromise she worked out allowed 68,400 acres for timber development, 1,099 acres for renewable-energy resources and recreational tourism projects, and 490 acres of Native cemetery and historic sites. She said on the floor that it would "help prevent the collapse of the timber industry in Southeast Alaska."

Resolution Copper was even more delicate and under negotiation for even longer—"nearly a decade," according to McCain. The company, part of a multinational giant, had bought up environmentally valuable land in anticipation of a land swap that would allow it to mine a huge copper deposit. But the mine is located on land that is sacred to the San Carlos Apaches, and the swap was opposed by environmentalists and the tribe. The parties finally reached a complicated agreement that laid the foundation for an economic boon in a depressed area. It had GOP support as well as backing from Democratic Representative Ann Kirkpatrick (thanked in a McCain press release a few months before she announced she would try—and ultimately fail—to win his Senate seat in 2016).

For Democrats, Sealaska and Resolution Copper were bitter pills. "Those are things we had fought for a long time. It's difficult to argue that the other little pieces that we got make up for those things," one Democrat said. "But we had to compare that list to what was likely to happen [after the 2014 election in a GOP-controlled Congress]. If you're realistic about that, the deal we struck was actually pretty good."

The Resolution Copper deal reverberated far beyond Arizona. A public-lands advocate who closely followed negotiations on the 2014 package called the copper mining agreement "the last piece of it. Finally there was some compromise on the way that was going to go. It was added and that made everything work."

THE DEVILISH DETAILS

Even so, the path to enactment was rocky from start to finish. From one day to the next, negotiators would go from "we're making tremendous progress" to "forget it," according to participants. "We kept blowing through deadlines. A lot of them," one said.

The main problem was trying to maintain delicate balances in a fluid situation. Each change of a number or a lawmaker's need would have a cascading effect. It was important that spending and revenues balanced out, but they were a moving target. "We would do our math properly only to find out that CBO [the Congressional Budget Office] had changed its mind" because of new information, a Republican negotiator recalled. "This was dead and was revived multiple times in about a week's period. We thought we'd solved a problem and then another one comes up."

The negotiators kept a tight grip on moneymaking items that could have passed the House and Senate on their own but were needed in the larger package to offset its costs. They also designated as an offset $70 million that compensates counties for federal land they aren't allowed to tax. They spread it across two years in order to keep each year revenue-neutral. "It all added up in the end," said one person who was at the table.

Balancing ideological wins for both sides was also complicated. There were new parks, wilderness areas and river protections, and those acres outnumbered the land opened for development and recreation. And "development" was defined loosely. For instance, a landlocked Utah town was given federal land to expand its cemetery. "That was a mark on the development side of the ledger," one Republican said, "but that's hardly development."

At the same time conservatives, scoring a big win for property owners, were able to rule out eminent domain as a tool in creating the newly protected parks, rivers and wilderness areas. "They were done in a way that gave Republicans less grief," said one GOP negotiator. "These were things that were resisted by the Democrats for a very long time, but we all have to give a little to get a little."

The resistance went both ways. "Wilderness issues with House Republicans were very contentious. They weren't enthusiastic about those," a Democratic negotiator said. "The House wanted to have a whole new set of management requirements that were very different from the past."

Ultimately, the Democrat said, success came down to "you got what you wanted in a version you were willing to live with, and that other thing you didn't want, we got it to where you could tolerate it."

Reid—whose Nevada achievements included both new copper mining and new wilderness—praised the end result as "a good compromise" that was "vitally important to America." Murkowski, finally able to move on from Sealaska-or-bust mode, lauded both the result and what she called a painstaking and traditional negotiation process. "We don't need to start over, working on the same bills in a new Congress," she said on the floor. "It's time to finish this."

The $585 billion NDAA, with its unexpected cache of public lands provisions, passed the House 300-119 on December 4 and the Senate approved it 89-11 on December 12. Obama signed it a week later without ceremony. Hastings framed his crowning achievement primarily in terms of its commercial impact. "This agreement is good for jobs and the economy," he said.

CONDITIONS RIPE FOR COMPROMISE

There was no shortage of regional and partisan tensions over how to handle federal lands, yet the atmosphere turned out to be ripe for successful negotiations. Many encouraging circumstances identified by the American Political Science Association were present in 2014 as the House and Senate got down to business.

Pressure was a prime motivator, starting with the demands that had built up during the five-year pause on wilderness and parks bills. The imminent retirements of key figures, including Hastings and Levin, added still more urgency. So did the fact that so many leadership figures, including chairmen and senior members of relevant committees, wanted to deliver on pet projects. Landrieu had only a minor personal stake in the lands package and was preoccupied right up through a December 6 runoff with what turned out to be a losing re-election campaign in Louisiana, but she wanted to accomplish whatever was possible.

Reid personally had lots he wanted to get done before the Senate changed hands, as it appeared likely to do, and assigned his staff to participate in the negotiations. "You can tell by the number of Nevada bills included that Senator Reid was front and center in pushing for this," said Mike Matz, director of U.S. Public Lands for the Pew Charitable Trusts. Reid's involvement was enormously helpful, he added: "At the end of a session, you've got to go with what's moving and what is going to get past both bodies. Frankly, Harry Reid is a master at this. He'd done it many times previously."

House Republican leaders were also keenly interested and kept in the loop. With the election approaching, they wanted members to have victories to talk about back home, and they also wanted to make sure the overall package could be sold to their caucus. Whatever deal emerged, one GOP negotiator said, had to "play by the rules of the House and House Republican protocols."

Murkowski and Hastings did not know each other before this negotiation. Some of the staff negotiators had longstanding professional relationships, but others started off as strangers. The House GOP-Senate majority leader interaction was especially unusual. "House Republicans sitting down at a table with Harry Reid folks. That's not something that happens often," one participant said. "We didn't know them very well before," said another. "We know them very well now," added a third.

This negotiation hinged more than many on career staffers. Members had informal conversations when necessary, such as to resolve sticking points, but they did not hold formal meetings to hammer out the package. A Democratic aide said that would have been impossible because there were so many moving pieces, and pointless because the pieces—having been through most or all of the legislative process—were well known to lawmakers. "Our bosses trusted us to work it out," the aide said.

Trust among the negotiators at the table took some time to develop. They shared a mutual bipartisan frustration about their inability to do their jobs—that is, to get their bills to the finish line. At the same time, however, "you doubt that the other side understands what it's going to take for you to be able to do something," a Republican said.

The negotiators not only figured that out, they kept their word to stay quiet about what they were doing. That was critical with a package of this size and complexity. Anyone who heard about it would want their bill included, and "you can't do everything," as one negotiator put it.

The code of silence was vital for that and many other reasons. "Any one of us could have derailed this had we wanted to by simply saying to the wrong person, and we'd know who that person would be, 'Here's what we're doing' or 'Can you believe x bill is in?'" a Republican negotiator explained. "The wrong person could have been a reporter. Or telling a member or someone on a member's staff, 'We're working on this package but guess what, your bill's not in.' Or 'Hey, that bill you really hate? Guess what, it's in.'"

The process was so private that Utah Senator Mike Lee and others would later accuse the negotiators of a secret plot. But in some ways they were operating in plain sight, obscured by a crush of year-end business that distracted the press and kept coverage to a minimum. "There's so much going on that you don't necessarily stand out," one aide said. Another called the degree of privacy shocking but also essential.

"Had the press gotten ahold of it, it wouldn't have worked," the aide said. "It was pretty crazy—once we had the package together and we knew it was going to be in, even then it wasn't in until it was in. And we had to lock arms on this because we knew what a lightning rod the whole deal could be regardless of which side of the aisle you were on. If the press started picking it apart … it had to be this or it had to be nothing."

COBURN'S LAST STAND

Close to 50 unhappy environmental groups pressed to have the lands package removed from the defense bill, but most of the major advocacy groups—also unhappy—accepted it as the best they could do. It was conservatives who were the most incensed and who mounted a last stand on the floor. They objected to both the content of the agreement and its presence as a hitchhiker on the defense bill.

Their standard bearer was the retiring Senator Tom Coburn of Oklahoma. "A bill that defines the needs of our nation's defense is hardly the proper place to trample on private property rights," Coburn had told Senate Minority Leader Mitch McConnell in a November letter. "Nor is it the place to restrict access to hunting, fishing and other recreational opportunities on massive swaths of taxpayer-supported lands."

In December, Coburn argued on the floor that expanding the national park system was a "disastrous" idea because "our parks are falling apart." We can have new parks, he said, "but we ought to have a plan to take care of the ones we have now before we add additional national parks and put at risk the most fantastic national park system in the world."

Coburn allies included Senator Ted Cruz of Texas, who called the lands package "an extreme land grab," and Utah's Lee, who called the NDAA "a legislative hodgepodge." Lee added: "Most egregiously, the drafters secretly added 68 unrelated bills pertaining to the use of federal lands." Ten conservative groups protested the package in a letter to House members, arguing among other things that the government should not own more land and that a proposed women's history museum would be offensive to the military.

The American Conservative Union and Heritage Action were among the organizations lining up in favor of a Coburn motion to strip the lands package. But the Senate rejected that idea, 82-18. It was a display of confidence in a deal and in a team of negotiators who had started off as skeptics and ended up as believers. "There was mutual distrust about whether we could get to an agreement," one Republican aide said. "But by the end, folks thought we had something fair and defensible."

The principal players went on to new phases of their lives and careers. Levin, McKeon and Hastings left Congress. Reid became the Senate minority leader and a lame duck. Bishop moved up to chair the House Natural Resources Committee, and Murkowski became chair of the Senate Energy and Natural Resources Committee.

In her new role, Murkowski soon announced another sweeping bipartisan deal, this one an energy policy modernization act in partnership with senior Washington state Democrat Maria Cantwell. As it moved through the committee, the Senate, the House and further rounds of negotiations, Murkowski would test the skills she had honed on the public lands deal of 2014. As she told Alaska Public Radio, explaining how that agreement had come to pass, "Finesse. It took finesse."

In Congress, however, the final chapter never seems to be written. The mine planned by Resolution Copper continued to draw protests and controversies, and several bills were introduced in 2016 to undo the land swap that had been a linchpin of the 2014 deal.

As for the Murkowski-Cantwell energy policy bill, the two parties had come to what Cantwell called hard-fought policy agreements on water, wildfires, sportsmen issues, hydroelectric and nuclear power, innovation, cybersecurity and management reforms. Murkowski said late in 2016 that all but two issues had been resolved. She accused her fellow Republicans in the House of "attempting to run us out of time, in order to prevent this bill from moving forward, even though it contains the priorities of dozens of its members."

There was, Murkowski said, plenty of time to work out House-Senate differences over the remaining couple of issues. Emboldened by Donald Trump's victory, however, House GOP leaders were not inclined toward compromise. They rushed home for the holidays in early December 2016 and the Murkowski-Cantwell bill died.

Would their work be for nothing? Probably not. But other congressional deal-making sagas suggest it could take years for their efforts to come to fruition.

CASE STUDY FOUR

A FARM-BILL FIRESTORM OVER FOOD STAMPS

Farmers usually don't see their policy fights make national headlines. But that was before the Tea Party came to town.

These upstart conservatives, carried to victory in the Republican midterm rout of 2010, had a distinctive profile. They wanted a much smaller government and much less spending. And they had a decidedly populist bent that announced they were not your father's business-oriented, country-club Republicans. They crusaded to cut what they viewed as corporate welfare payouts as well as programs for poor and low-income Americans.

Some of the pressure yielded fruit in the form of bipartisan changes to farm subsidy programs that many in both parties understood had evolved in ways that were very difficult to justify. And some of the pressure yielded the opposite—a pitched battle over food stamps that thrust the farm bill into the thick of the red-blue culture wars and a charged 2012 campaign-trail debate over government dependency.

Over years of talks that began in 2011, as a recession and demands for tax-and-spending cuts shrank the size of the federal pie, battles over the agriculture budget were a constant. Team Corn-and-Beans (the Midwest) was slugging it out with Team Cotton-Rice-and-Peanuts (the South) in a competition for federal payments. And, in customary farm-bill tradition, conflicts within the dairy industry were among the last to be resolved.

But it was the Supplemental Nutrition Assistance Program (better known as food stamps or SNAP), the largest single item in the federal agriculture budget, that became a lightning rod for attention, amendments and ideological point-making. Drug-testing, work requirements and huge benefit cuts were all in the mix. And it was an explosive mix indeed. Lawmakers finally managed to defuse it in February 2014, ending a 16-month cycle of expirations and extensions of a 2008 farm law.

The final product was a departure in a number of ways. It made unusually substantial cuts in payments to farmers. In addition, geography—the traditional dividing line among farm-bill factions—was overtaken by ideology. "The partisanship around food stamps added a massive twist to the normal farm bill process," said one

Democrat involved in the negotiations.

The 2014 farm bill was also a relative rarity for its time because of the route it took to enactment. It was not an agreement reached in private by a handful of people that was then presented as a done deal to the rank and file. In contrast to that mode of doing business, so prevalent in an era of gridlock, it was close to a textbook example of "how a bill becomes a law."

It went through the agriculture committees in the Republican House and the Democratic Senate, then it went to the House and Senate floors. People had a chance to vote on amendments. Then the differing bills went to a House-Senate conference committee. The conferees and their staffs negotiated their way to a compromise, which then passed both chambers and went to President Obama's desk.

A CYCLE OF CRISES

"It's a good sign that Democrats and Republicans in Congress were able to come through with this bill, break the cycle of short-sighted, crisis-driven partisan decision-making, and actually get this stuff done," Obama said as he signed the bill into law at Michigan State University in East Lansing. "And that's the way you should expect Washington to work."

It was indeed a good sign, but it came only after years of stressful detours and dead ends. "I have been here for seven of these five-year farm bills, and I have never seen such a roller coaster in my life," Vermont Senator Patrick Leahy said at a press conference a few days before the signing.

There were many factors working against a farm-bill compromise. On the politics front alone, there were the demands of Tea Party rebels, many of them impatient political novices, and the inability of Republican leaders to corral their votes or rhetoric. Additional complications included heavy press coverage of parts of the process, and heavy involvement by some top congressional leaders. There was also major pressure from agriculture sectors that saw cuts in their future, and in the 2013-14 act of the saga, there was a Senate personnel change that brought new demands from Southern farmers.

All of those conditions are inhospitable to negotiations, according to research conducted by the American Political Science Association (APSA). But at the same time, there were reasons to believe those at the table would succeed. While food stamps made headlines, some of the heaviest lifting on esoteric but equally controversial matters was done in private. Most of the aides working on nuts and bolts were familiar with each other. That was true of some of their bosses, as well. And those principals—Representatives Frank Lucas of Oklahoma and Collin Peterson of Minnesota and Senators Debbie Stabenow of Michigan, Pat Roberts of Kansas and Thad Cochran of Mississippi—agreed on at least a few things.

There was, for instance, widespread acknowledgment—if reluctant in some quarters—of the need to trim spending on both food stamps and commodity support programs. There was also a shared persistence on display as farm-bill talks launched and relaunched in 2011, 2012 and 2013, and a large body of work from earlier rounds that gave negotiators a substantial head start as they repeatedly geared up.

Then there was what farm groups viewed as their failsafe: An underlying 1949 farm bill that had never been repealed. That's what takes effect unless a new farm bill is passed or extended every five years. The consequences of reverting to a 65-year-old law would be dire, topped by a plunge off the "dairy cliff"—shorthand for 1940s policies that would drive up milk prices to $7 per gallon. It was the perfect penalty default—the term APSA uses for bipartisan fear of failure, typically a top motivator in negotiations that succeed.

A DIVERSE CAST

The new lead player in the long-running farm-bill drama was Stabenow, a veteran member of the Senate Agriculture Committee who in 2011 became the first woman to chair it. A low-key Michigan Democrat with underestimated political skills, she won her first election at age 24. According to *The Almanac of American Politics*, she defeated a county commissioner who called her "that young broad." Her home state is known for its auto industry, but agriculture is one of its top three industries and accounts for more than 20 percent of Michigan jobs. The state's diverse crops range from corn and soybeans to fruits and vegetables. It's also the nation's third-largest producer of Christmas trees.

The GOP House sweep of 2010 propelled Lucas to the agriculture chairmanship in 2011. An understated farmer and rancher with a pragmatic mindset on farm issues, he faced challenges posed by new members who were dead set on spending cuts, disinterested in bipartisanship and unfamiliar with the rural-urban coalition that often helped farm bills succeed. They were, he would say, young pups who had to be educated, and that education took a while.

Lucas himself represents the most Republican district in Oklahoma, as measured by the Cook Partisan Voting Index. But he had a close working relationship with Peterson, a former committee chairman who was its senior Democrat during the 2011-2014 farm-bill process. The veteran Minnesota congressman, an expert on dairy issues, was the one of the rare conservatives in his party who kept his seat throughout the Obama administration. He played guitar with other lawmakers in the Second Amendments rock band and was an accountant by trade—a skill he used to keep tabs on pain and gain during farm bill talks.

The two other main players were Roberts in 2011-12 and Cochran in 2013-14. The two long-serving Senate Republicans were both old hands at writing farm bills—Cochran had chaired the committee in 2003-2005—but this was the first time they were legislating with the Tea Party looking over their shoulders. With the advent of the new GOP majority in 2011, "the entire emphasis of so many members was 100 percent deficit reduction come hell or high water," one Republican recalled. "There were no real substantive conversations about anything but cut, cut, cut, cut, cut."

THE SUPER COMMITTEE — 2011

Stabenow had been in charge of the Senate agriculture committee for just a few months when Congress and the White House struck a deal to head off a debt-ceiling disaster: A "super committee" of 12 senators and representatives, officially named the Joint Committee on Deficit Reduction, had to come up with $1.2 trillion in budget cuts over 10 years or else an across-the-board cut, or sequester, would take effect at year-end. All House and Senate committees were asked to recommend cuts that would avert the dreaded sequester.

Many farmers and their allies liked the 2008 farm bill and would have been happy to simply extend it. But Stabenow went in with guns blazing, as one negotiator put it. She saw the super committee request as an opening to propose big changes. Her chief negotiating partners were Lucas and Peterson, and there was "at least some buy-in" from all three on major issues, one aide said. Roberts, however, was "an outlier" at times. "What really pushed him to the sidelines a little bit was where we ended up landing on the commodity programs. He was not a big fan," the aide said.

The first challenge for the negotiators was to figure out the size of a credible overall cut and how much would come from each main section of the farm bill: commodities, conservation and nutrition. They settled on a topline reduction of $23 billion over 10 years, including $7 billion from food stamps; $4 billion from conservation programs, and $12 billion from commodity supports.

The easiest decision was to streamline the conservation programs that helped farmers protect drinking water, reduce soil erosion, preserve forests, wetlands and wildlife habitat, and repair damage from natural disasters. The negotiators achieved savings by consolidating 23 programs into 13—a plan that survived in its basic form right up through the 2014 compromise that was signed into law.

Food stamps were not subject to the sequester, and the super committee wasn't considering cuts to them. The overriding Democratic goal was to protect the program—and yet the farm-committee Democrats decided to propose a cut. "We had to do something or we were never going to get these guys to do anything" on commodities, one negotiator said. "The vast majority [of savings] came from direct payments. We had to do something reciprocal on our priorities, which was SNAP."

The cut was achieved largely by limiting the ability of states to link SNAP benefits with the Low Income Home Energy Assistance Program (LIHEAP)—another idea that made it into law three years later. Some states were giving people small amounts of heating aid, sometimes as tiny as 10 cents or $1 a year, which allowed them to receive increased food benefits even if they hadn't actually paid high utility costs. Congress had established this linkage in federal law as a way to reduce paperwork and improve efficiency. But Republicans and Democrats agreed that, in practice, some states were flouting congressional intent and undermining the program.

From the Democratic perspective, it was the least bad way to wring savings from SNAP. Fewer people would qualify for higher benefits, but nobody would lose what they were already getting. "We felt that was a little bit of a budget gimmick. It didn't affect people's monthly allowance. None of the policy had to do with new standards" for eligibility, one negotiator said.

Stabenow had said from the outset that it was time to end the system of direct payments to commodity farmers and landowners, which was costing some $5 billion a year. "Those payments went out no matter what. High prices, low prices. Good crops, bad crops. It had become indefensible," said a GOP aide involved in the negotiations. Not only were members under intense pressure to cut spending, the farm economy was booming. "We're going to record farm incomes and these payments are still going out. There's no trigger on them. You don't have to have a loss. You don't have to have low prices. It was going to be very difficult if not impossible to sustain politically," said another GOP aide.

Roberts had written the direct payment system in 1996 and was not happy about making changes, but most in Congress saw little alternative from a political standpoint. Against a drumbeat of Tea Party attacks on wasteful spending and corporate welfare, Lucas and Peterson joined Stabenow in creating a new, two-pronged safety net. Farmers could sign up for payments triggered by either a drop in the price of a crop or a drop in revenue for any reason. They would kick in when there were losses as determined by a pre-set formula. The bill also tightened the definition of "active farmer," the term used to determine who was eligible for subsidies.

Stabenow likes to boast that the House and Senate agriculture committees produced the only bipartisan, bicameral recommendation to the super committee. But it never went anywhere—in fact, it was never even released to the public—because the super committee collapsed in November 2011. Roberts issued a statement saying Stabenow and Lucas had drafted the bill behind closed doors, "largely without my input." He said he was concerned about the commodity changes and how the spending reductions had been allocated, and looked forward to a normal, more open farm-bill process.

A Senate Triumph — June 2012

The 2011 proposal nevertheless proved to be a solid foundation on which to build. "It set the framework of negotiations for the next three years," said a Democrat involved in the talks. The hard work of determining the size of an overall cut had been done, and the structural reforms to conservation and commodities provided a surprisingly durable blueprint. Nutrition, namely food stamps, was where things kept going off the rails.

The Senate process was relatively smooth. Stabenow and Roberts wrote the bill together, preserving the $23 billion in savings, the conservation consolidation and the new commodity-payment structure from 2011. In addition, they strengthened a crop insurance program that Roberts said was the top priority for virtually every producer who testified before the committee (insurance programs require premium payments, and benefits are not automatic but rather triggered by losses). They also cracked down on fraud and abuse in the food-stamp program for a savings of $4 billion. That included limits on the LIHEAP-SNAP link modeled on those in the 2011 super committee proposal.

The bill came out of committee on a bipartisan 16-5 vote, then passed the Senate on a bipartisan vote of 64-35 after a two-day marathon of votes on 73 floor amendments. Stabenow called it "the greatest reform in agriculture in decades." Farmers, she said, would no longer be paid for crops they don't grow, or acres they don't plant, or when they are doing well. Actual price or yield drops would trigger a safety net, she said, and broader crop insurance would protect farmers against weather disasters.

Roberts, the outlier on commodities in 2011, had come around. He noted on the floor that he understood the elimination of direct payments was "a big deal" to Kansas wheat-growers and other commodity producers. But he said the committee was not picking winners and losers or undermining the farm safety net. "Money is shifting among commodities because farmers are farming differently," he said. He also noted that "the taxpayers have been clear in this budget climate" that Congress should not "continue and defend" the program.

Senate Majority Leader Harry Reid credited Stabenow and Roberts with the win. He said he and minority leader Mitch

McConnell had been "bystanders to much of what's gone on. It's been the work of these two fine senators and the cooperation of every member." After the vote, one GOP aide recalled, members from both parties—even some who voted against the final bill—rushed up to thank Stabenow and Roberts for the chance to vote on amendments.

Stabenow and Roberts were driven in part by the fear that if they didn't produce a bill, agriculture would become part of a massive year-end deal to avoid a series of fiscal nightmares known as the "fiscal cliff." They wanted a bipartisan bill, not one that was molded by hard-core conservatives or people less familiar with farm programs, one Republican said. Their view was that "if we can't do this on our own, they're going to do it to us, so let's do it when we have the control."

FOOD STAMP DRAMA — LATE 2012

The House Agriculture Committee also produced a bipartisan farm bill, approved 35-11 in July 2012. But things quickly disintegrated. Every member of the House was up for re-election, and Republicans were under pressure to be as conservative as possible. Food stamps, meanwhile, were an incendiary and continuing theme in the GOP presidential primary campaign. Former House speaker Newt Gingrich often called Obama "the food stamp president" and made the incorrect claim that the nation's first black president had put more people on food stamps than any president in U.S. history. He also said on the campaign trail that "the African-American community should demand paychecks and not be satisfied with food stamps."

Food stamps were not born to this kind of political controversy. They had long been a weapon against hunger, deployed on and off in pilot programs from the Great Depression until 1964, when President Lyndon Johnson established a national food-stamp program as part of his War on Poverty. And they had always been linked to farm programs, because they began with the government buying surplus commodities and food to feed the poor in cities, suburbs and rural America.

The modern program dates from a 1977 reform act pushed by two farm-state senators who had spent a decade investigating hunger in

America. "We worked hand in glove. We didn't play any partisanship with this issue," George McGovern, the late South Dakota Democrat, says of himself and Republican Bob Dole of Kansas in a 2011 video released by the Dole Institute of Politics at the University of Kansas. The main reform of the 1977 act was to eliminate a requirement that Americans pay for a portion of their food stamps. "If you didn't have that money to put up, then you weren't eligible for the program. It didn't make any sense to me," Dole said in the video.

The program, now known as SNAP, was a boon to children, the elderly, the disabled and workers with low-wage jobs. It also became a boon for the farm bill by creating a well of support among urban lawmakers who wouldn't necessarily be fans of federal aid to agriculture. That was not a dynamic familiar to some Tea Party newcomers who were chomping at the bit to slash SNAP. "They had not been around and didn't understand how you built broader support than just rural ag-state members," one Republican aide said.

What they did understand was that during the Great Recession, the SNAP program had grown massively—from 28.2 million people and $37.6 billion in 2008, the first full year of recession, to 47.6 million people and nearly $80 billion in 2013, a period of declining wages and a lethargic recovery. Part of the added cost came from easing sign-up procedures for states. Part came from Obama's 2009 stimulus package, which temporarily increased monthly benefits by between $2 and $24 per person for several years.

"To put it in context, the program doubled in cost over the span of eight years," a GOP negotiator said. "Absolutely some of it was because of the recession. But it still far exceeded what levels you could point to as being recession-related."

Not surprisingly, House conservatives demanded major cuts and restructuring. Some were enamored of a 2012 Heritage Foundation paper that called food stamps "an expensive, old-style entitlement program that discourages work, rewards idleness, and promotes long-term dependence." The authors said SNAP should be turned into "a work activation program"—that is, able-bodied SNAP recipients should have to work, prepare for work or at least look for work as a condition of receiving aid. They also proposed a spending cap that would save $150 billion over 10 years and end SNAP's status as an entitlement program serving all who qualified.

Heritage further called for mandatory drug testing of food-stamp beneficiaries. People getting help from taxpayers "should engage in responsible and constructive behavior as a condition of receiving aid," the group said. Stabenow's view of drug testing was simple. She said she'd consider it as soon as tests were required for farmers who received federal help.

House Republican leaders did not have the votes to pass a bill, so they never brought one to the floor. The Senate bill died, and on October 1, 2012, the 2008 law expired. "The excitement that is the farm bill process," Dale Moore, executive director for public policy at the American Farm Bureau, said dryly.

As New Year's Eve 2012 became New Year's Day 2013, Congress approved a fiscal cliff deal that extended the 2008 farm law until Sepember. 30, 2013. It was, aides reflected later, probably unrealistic to think they could pass something as big as a farm bill during a presidential election year.

STARTING ALL OVER AGAIN — 2013

The 2012 elections did not transform the political landscape of divided government. When Congress returned in 2013, Democrats still controlled the White House and the Senate, and Republicans still controlled the House. By then, there had been so much House turnover that more than half the members had never before dealt with a farm bill.

There had been one major shift in Senate personnel: Cochran exercised his seniority over Roberts to replace him as the senior Republican on the agriculture committee. He had "timed out" as the senior Republican on the appropriations committee and decided Southern agriculture needed more of a voice on the farm panel.

That led to more than two months of negotiations to raise subsidy payments and strengthen insurance for Southern crops, resulting in a bill with strong support from the region. Overall the Senate's 2013 farm bill saved $24 billion over 10 years. The savings followed similar patterns as in 2012, including $4.1 billion from the SNAP program, and the new bill passed by a similarly sweeping, bipartisan 66-27 vote.

Over in the House, the Tea Party contingent had grown. There were fewer Democrats from rural districts, and some of the

Republicans who replaced them were in the classic Tea Party mold. "There was a huge learning curve for those types who just read Heritage blogs and listened to talk radio," one Republican aide said. "Even though they lived in rural areas, they hated the farm programs."

Given the antipathy of Tea Party conservatives to SNAP, it was no surprise that the 2013 House agriculture committee bill achieved half its $40 billion in cuts from food stamps. That was nearly five times the savings proposed by the Senate. Democrats were split on the bill; the committee approved it in May on a bipartisan vote of 36 to 10.

On the House floor the next month, there ensued what Moore, the farm bureau official, called a "chutes and ladders game." Lawmakers considered some 100 amendments—highly atypical for the House— and then, to the shock of many, the bill went down to defeat, 234-195. Lucas and Peterson thought they had more than enough support to prevail. But they lost 62 Republicans and every Democrat.

Some Democrats were furious about what one Republican negotiator called "bumper-sticker" SNAP amendments that had been adopted as a group in the middle of the night. Examples included requiring drug testing as part of the SNAP application process and banning convicted murderers, pedophiles and rapists from the program ("not their children, not their spouses, but they themselves," Lucas emphasized later). The crowning outrage for Democrats was a work requirement that originated with then-Majority Leader Eric Cantor and became known as the Southerland amendment, after Representative Steve Southerland of Florida.

It allowed states to require most adults, including parents of children as young as a year old, to work or participate in a work or training program for at least 20 hours a week or lose their SNAP benefits. "It would also allow states to keep half of the federal savings from cutting people off, which state politicians would be allowed to use for any purpose, including *tax cuts and special-interest subsidies*," analysts at the liberal Center for Budget and Policy Priorities wrote—italics theirs.

Cantor made a rare speech praising the amendment and, though it passed on a voice vote, Southerland insisted on a recorded vote— ensuring that voters would know exactly who had been for and against the work requirement. "Democrats thought he spiked the football a little bit," a Republican negotiator said of Cantor. It was the last straw for them. Peterson said he had warned Cantor beforehand that "the timing was terrible" and he was worried about losing Democratic votes. "If you overreach, you get nothing," he said when they in fact deserted and the bill died.

. After the vote, House Minority Whip Steny Hoyer called the Cantor-Southerland amendment "a draconian amendment that would have hurt the poorest citizens in our country very badly. So we turned a bipartisan bill into a partisan bill." Cantor responded that SNAP was "in dire need of improvement" due to waste and error rates. "In addition to that," he said, "it reflects our strong belief that able-bodied people should have the opportunity and should go in and be a productive citizen."

The Two-Step House Solution — Summer 2013

Lucas, looking at an August recess followed by a September 30 expiration of the 2008 farm bill amid yet another federal budget crisis, solved his problem by splitting the bill in two. In July, he brought to the floor a farm bill that established a 10-year, $195 billion safety net for farmers and agribusiness and said not a word about food stamps. It passed on a party-line vote of 216 to 208, leaving anger and confusion in its wake. The bill, though it ended automatic direct payments to farmers, did not cut other subsidies enough to satisfy some conservatives. And liberals were furious about the missing food programs.

The House did come back in September and pass a nutrition bill—and it cut $40 billion from food stamps alone. That was double the cut in the defeated House farm bill and 10 times more than the SNAP savings in the Senate bill. The Congressional Budget Office estimated the new larger cuts would cause 3.8 million people to lose benefits in 2014.

Nearly $19 billion of the House's $40 billion in food-stamp savings came from limiting benefits for jobless adults without children to three months out of every three years, even if they couldn't find work. That was a change from the existing system, under which states could seek temporary waivers of the work requirement for adults in high-unemployment areas. Many governors in both parties had requested the waivers during the recession.

The nutrition-only bill was a depressing turn for Peterson, who had been working on a new farm bill for nearly four years. He said it was even worse than the defeated, comprehensive committee bill that had been "hijacked with partisan amendments" because it included all of those and went even further by cutting off the state waiver option. "There is a lot of hypocrisy coming from the other side of the aisle here," Peterson said.

Conservatives viewed Democrats as sticking their heads in the sand when it came to abuses in the food-stamp program. One Republican negotiator said the conflict stemmed not just from GOP insistence on massive cuts but also from "the Democrats' inability to even contemplate some of the incredibly egregious things states are doing inside the SNAP program. Beyond LIHEAP, both sides just dug in."

When Lucas finally spoke, he said he had been proud of the bipartisan bills his committee produced in 2012 and 2013. He pleaded with the House to pass the nutrition-only bill so that its reform ideas could be discussed in conference committee and perhaps included in a final compromise. "It should not be this hard to pass a bill to make sure that the consumers in this country and around the world have enough to eat," Lucas concluded. "It shouldn't be this hard, but everything seems to be hard these days. So let's do the hard things. Let's get our work done."

The $40 billion in SNAP cuts passed 217 to 210. Fifteen Republicans bucked their party and voted no. Not a single Democrat voted yes.

BRIDGING THE DIVIDE — LATE 2013

The farm-bill conference started in August with staff meetings and went right through January. The Democrats started from the position that House negotiators weren't going to get a dollar more on SNAP cuts than the $4.1 billion in the Senate bill and that there would be no "extracurricular issues" (such as controversial House policy riders on food stamps).

When it came to the math of the SNAP cuts, the two sides were not as far apart as they seemed. Senate Democrats, despite their opening bluster, agreed to double the cuts in their bill by further tightening the LIHEAP loophole. And House Republican negotiators understood that the $40 billion figure "was never real. It was an exercise we had to go through to get to conference. There was never a real conversation about it in conference," one Republican said. A Senate negotiator said there were hints from the start that the House "could pull off a farm bill with SNAP cuts more in our direction."

One bottom line was that Cochran, the senior Senate Republican, was never on board with $40 billion or anywhere close. His state of Mississippi had high poverty levels and high SNAP usage. He understood that "people aren't excited to be on the SNAP program but it is a viable way for them and their children to get the nutrition they need," a Republican negotiator said. Another negotiator recalled that Cochran "would come in and say the things he had to say, that we need to cut some fat out of the program to make it work better for those in need. But he never, ever, ever pushed us for the extreme cuts the House was pushing or even some of his own Senate colleagues were pushing. He just turned a quiet blind eye to a lot of it."

There was broad bipartisan agreement on trying to clean up fraud, abuse and inefficiency in SNAP. The conference agreement included many such provisions from both chambers, including making sure that lottery winners, affluent college students and liquor stores couldn't participate in SNAP, and cracking down on benefit trafficking by retailers and recipients. The final compromise did not sever the link some states had established between LIHEAP and SNAP, as Republicans would have liked. But it did raise the minimum for eligibility so that $1 heating checks could no longer trigger increased SNAP benefits.

The hot-button amendments, viewed by Democrats as "demeaning and offensive," in Leahy's words, posed another set of challenges. Many of them were omitted or watered down. The conferees rejected the House drug-testing requirement and softened a provision that would have slapped a lifetime SNAP ban on people convicted of a violent crime, even if they had paid their debt to society and become law-abiding citizens. On the big-ticket House eligibility provisions, negotiators rejected a change that would have cut off more than 2 million people with disposable family income below the poverty line. They also kept the state option to waive work requirements in areas with few jobs. And the Southerland-Cantor work amendment was changed into a pilot program affecting far fewer people.

"There was a group within the Republican conference that was pushing for a different agenda, a different number—one that was not going to pass the Senate let alone be signed by the president," said Moore, from the farm bureau. He said the tea leaves could be read from the start when Cochran made clear that "his number was somewhere in the $8 billion range." That is where the conferees ended up. It was also close to where Stabenow and Lucas had started in their super committee blueprint of 2011.

By January 2014, negotiators were down to a few final issues. One was to nail down the definition of an "actively engaged" farmer, the standard used to determine who was eligible for federal payments. "The system gets gamed," one negotiator said. "Your brothers and sisters can become partners and get subsidies, even if they're teachers and accountants." Some people helped manage more than one farming operation and claimed to be "actively engaged" in all of them. The negotiators agreed on some limits, and the agriculture secretary was authorized to work out the language.

THE FINAL FRONTIER — JANUARY 2014

The very last argument was over dairy policy, which is almost always the very last argument in a farm-bill negotiation. It was not particularly relevant to some people—as one aide noted, "You could fit all the dairy cows in Frank Lucas's district in the hearing room at the agriculture committee"—but to others it was critical. Two in the latter category were Peterson and House Speaker John Boehner, who jumped into the thick of negotiations.

Under the existing system, the federal government bought milk, cheese and butter if prices fell below certain levels. Peterson wanted to offer farmers a government insurance plan to guarantee a certain margin between feed costs and milk prices and a "market stabilization" program of government incentives to reduce production when prices drop.

Boehner had long fought what he called "Soviet-style" dairy supports and dismissed the stabilization plan as more centralized government control. "I've fought off the supply and management ideas for 23 years that I have been in Congress, and my position hasn't changed," he said at a press conference. The dispute pitted Boehner and his allies, large food processors such as Kraft and Nestle, against dairy farmers, Senate negotiators who had adopted the Peterson plan, and Peterson himself—a farm-bill veteran described by one staff negotiator as "a prairie populist first and foremost."

The National Milk Producers Federation blamed Boehner for threats that killed Peterson's "stabilization" incentives. But it wasn't a total loss since a version of Peterson's margin insurance plan did make it into law. "The milk glass is more than half-full," group president Jim Mulhern said.

Leahy, who was deeply involved in the negotiations, described the level of intensity after the fact. "Senator Stabenow and I were on the phone or emailing about every hour of the day, night, and weekends from Michigan, Vermont, overseas, and from the Senate, but it worked," he said on the floor. "Everybody had a chance, Republicans and Democrats alike, to express their views."

And so in the end, for all the food-stamp headlines and angst, it was a dairy dispute that held up the farm bill. The conference report finally passed the House 251-166 on January 29, 2014, and the Senate 68-32 less than a week later. "Aside from the food-stamp mess," one aide said, "it was tinkering with the template from 2011."

How They Did It

The Agricultural Act of 2014 was the product of a rare bipartisan collaboration that once was the norm on Capitol Hill. Against the backdrop of the highly polarized and ideological Congresses of the past few years, the odds of that looked dim, but there were some classic conditions that suggested a compromise might emerge.

Calendar pressure was the most obvious. For three years farm negotiators were faced with a rolling series of deadlines, crises and expirations—from the 2011 super committee process and impending sequestration, to the expiration of the 2008 farm bill on September 30, 2012, and the fiscal cliff at year's end, to a farm-bill extension that expired on September 30, 2013, for most crops and ended for the rest on December 31. For reformers, whether they wanted changes in food stamps, commodity subsidies, conservation programs, dairy supports or any combination, there was never a good time to let up. The pressures and opportunities peaked as 2014 began with no modern farm law on the books.

It helped as the farm-bill saga dragged on that some divides were regional rather than partisan and that some coalitions cut across party lines—such as the aversion to "corporate welfare" (farm subsidies) shared by Tea Party conservatives, urban Democrats and the Heritage Foundation.

Some of the lawmakers and staff doing the negotiating knew each other well, but some did not. Some were involved in every round of negotiation from 2011 to 2014. Cochran's ascent to ranking member created a new dynamic with Stabenow. The pair's aides huddled in August 2013 to get to know each other, lay out their bosses' interests, and identify the poison pills that would kill any chance at cooperation.

Stabenow's personality was an important factor throughout the years of negotiations. "She was just an energizer bunny. She would call anybody. She wore people down," one Republican aide said. Another Republican called her "a very hands-on negotiator" and added, with a laugh, "Whenever I saw her, she had plenty of things to convey. There's nothing wrong with that."

Cochran put a priority on getting to know Stabenow, and he wanted his staff to get to know her staff. One aide said Cochran had an "old-school" approach: "You get to know people and you get to trust them and then you can negotiate and do it in a positive way on solid ground."

To that end, Cochran invited Stabenow to appear with him in Cleveland, Mississippi, at the annual meeting of the Delta Council in May 2013. It was an education in Southern agriculture for a Midwestern senator, and a revelation for her audience. Tommy Horton, editor of a publication called *Cotton Farming*, called Stabenow's speech "nothing short of remarkable" and praised her and Cochran for improving the treatment of Southern commodities in their farm bill that year.

Both sides in the years of negotiations said there were combative moments. One negotiator said that "the key people were cordial and professional," but added that "we didn't make a lot of friends in this process. There was not a lot of staff sitting around having beers together." Nor did ideology remain outside the room. "We felt pretty strongly that our side was more righteous and they felt the same," one Democrat said.

One thing the two sides shared was pressure. "There were multiple occasions of administration people—USDA people or lobbyists or other people—coming to us and saying 'You guys have done such a great job, you just need to close it out,'" one Democrat said. "It was their way of saying, 'just cave.'"

On the GOP side, negotiators were dealing with Cantor's deep involvement in SNAP work requirements and Boehner's strong feelings on dairy programs. "I don't even remember what the dairy compromise was and how this dairy program actually works," a Republican aide said later. "It was higher profile than it needed to be because of the speaker's involvement."

Unlike some negotiations that can be handled mostly by staff, farm issues required heavy participation by the four top members of the two agriculture committees. One GOP aide described the process this way: "The staff gets in a room, pounds the table, yells at each other and calls each other names. They come to an agreement on some things and agree to work on other things. Then they get to a third bucket of things and it's 'This is going to have to be a member decision, we're never going to get there.'

"I couldn't tell you how many principal meetings of the Big Four, but there were a lot," the aide added. "That is when the big sticking points would be litigated" on food stamps, dairy supports, commodity trigger points, and who counts as an "actively engaged" farmer.

The negotiators encountered considerable skepticism, especially in the final round after Republicans had passed a SNAP bill that Democrats and even some Republicans viewed as punitive. Democrats were well aware that Lucas, in his first big leadership position, wanted to show he could get a farm bill across the finish line. But he was in a tough spot on food stamps, caught between the Heritage wing of his party on one side and Obama and Senate Democrats on the other.

Conservative demands on food stamps ultimately gave way to forging a bill capable of passing the Senate and winning Obama's signature. "He knew the right flank was never going to be happy and never going to pass a bill for him," one Democrat said of Lucas. That analysis was borne out in the final tally when 63 House

Republicans, many of them identified with the Tea Party, voted no. They considered its SNAP reforms far too modest.

SNAP in fact began to shrink soon after passage of the farm law, but that was primarily due to the nation's continued recovery from recession. "Changes in the economy are having much more impact than changes in policy," said Moore, the farm bureau official.

The people who worked on the law concede that the food-stamp debate "certainly went to a new level of animosity," as one longtime GOP aide put it, from 2011 to 2013. But they and their bosses remain proud of what they ultimately accomplished both in substance (badly needed reforms and savings) and process (a traditional journey through committees and amendments).

"I have the signed bill on my wall at my office," one aide said. "It's surprising that it went the way it should have gone. A lot of committees don't have that ability anymore."

ACKNOWLEDGEMENTS

This book would not have been possible without the creative inspiration of Elaine Kamarck, the godmother of the original Brookings "Profiles in Negotiations" series, as I've described in the preface. I must also thank Walter Shapiro for inviting me to be his co-writer on an earlier Kamarck-inspired project, an analysis of the 2014 House primaries, and for his unerring guidance on everything from column topics to career paths.

I'm indebted to, among many others, newly elected Senator Chris Van Hollen of Maryland, who was a senior House Democrat on budget policy in 2013 and offered valuable insights into the Murray-Ryan negotiations; Nina Easton of *Fortune*, who helped me find the Patty Murray video that ignited Elaine's imagination; investigative reporter Dennis Wagner of *The Arizona Republic*; Ian DePlanque of the American Legion; Republican Fred Ferguson, a congressional aide and lands expert; Mike Matz, director of U.S. Public Lands for the Pew Charitable Trusts; Dale Moore of the American Farm Bureau; Katherine A. Scott, the Senate historian who tipped me off to the public-lands deal, a fascinating saga that had unfolded in secret; the Paul Ryan aide who tracked down what kind of fish Ryan liked to catch; and all the other Capitol Hill aides who unearthed information and trusted me to tell their stories in a balanced and factual way.

Finally, I must thank my husband, John Martin—my funny, wise and cherished life partner; an impeccable editor and first reader; a critic when it's needed and a cheerleader when it's deserved; and a man who has put up with a lot, including my consuming (and no doubt disturbing) fixation on politics.

ABOUT THE AUTHOR

Jill Lawrence became commentary editor of *USA Today* in January 2016. A columnist for *USA Today* and a former columnist for Creators Syndicate, *U.S. News & World Report* and the Associated Press, she has won National Press Club, Sigma Delta Chi and National Headliner awards for her writing.

Lawrence is the co-author of "Governors and the Presidency: How They Campaign, How They Govern," for the Eagleton Institute of Politics at Rutgers, and "Phoning It In and Failing to Show: The Story of the 2014 House Primaries," for the Brookings Institution. She also is a contributor to *The Surge: 2014's Big GOP Win and What It Means for the Next Presidential Race.*

She has covered every presidential campaign since 1988, as well as historic events such as the 1998 Clinton impeachment, the 2000 Florida recount and the health-reform battles of the Clinton and Obama eras. Her positions have included managing editor for politics at *National Journal*, senior correspondent at AOL's *Politics Daily*, national political correspondent at *USA Today*, and national political writer for the AP. Her work has also appeared online in *Politico Magazine, The Week, The Daily Beast* and *The Atlantic*.

Columbia Journalism Review named Lawrence one of the top 10 campaign reporters in the country in 2004, when she covered Democratic nominee John Kerry for *USA Today*. *Washingtonian* magazine included her on its list of 50 "best and most influential journalists" in 2005.

A highlight of her earlier tenure at *USA Today* was "One Nation, Divided," a series which she proposed after the stalemated 2000 election and which ran in 2002. The stories were based on research and reporting throughout 2001, both before and after the 9/11 attacks, in the archetypal blue and red towns of Montclair, New Jersey, and Franklin, Tennessee. In 2003, the *IRE Journal* published an article she wrote about how and why the towns were chosen and the tools she used to dig out the information she needed.

Lawrence has a master's degree in journalism from New York University and a bachelor's degree in music literature from the University of Michigan. She lives in Washington, D.C., with her husband, John, an editor. They have two sons, one a violinist and the other a screenwriter and composer.

Made in the USA
Monee, IL
06 July 2022

99127007R00049